# GONORRHEA

# AND

# SYPHILIS

## *(1912)*

A DRUGLESS TREATMENT
OF VENEREAL DISEASES
BY THE FAMED
DR. TILDEN

## J.H. Tilden

ISBN 1-56459-875-6

# Kessinger Publishing's Rare Reprints
## Thousands of Scarce and Hard-to-Find Books!

- •
- •
- •
- •
- •
- •
- •
- •
- •
- •
- •
- •
- •
- •
- •
- •
- •
- •
- •

We kindly invite you to view our extensive catalog list at:
http://www.kessinger.net

# Warning—Disclaimer

# Preface

Dr. John H. Tilden, the son of a physician, was born in Van Burenburg, Illinois, on January 21, 1851. He received his medical education at the Eclectic Medical Institute, Cincinnati, Ohio, a medical school founded in 1830 as a protest against the allopathic and homeopathic schools of medicine of that time. He was graduated in 1872, with the degree of doctor of medicine. From the best information we can obtain, his father was a Dr. Joseph G. Tilden, who came from Vermont in 1837 to Kentucky, in which State he married.

Dr. John H. Tilden started the practice of medicine at Nokomis, Illinois, then for a year at St. Louis, Missouri, and then at Litchfield, Illinois, until 1890, when he moved to Denver, Colorado. In Denver he located in the downtown business section, in an office with other doctors. Later he established a sanitarium in an outer section of the city. This sanitarium and school he conducted until 1924, when he sold the Institution, for about half of what he had plowed back into its development, to a Dr. Arthur Voss of Cincinnati, Ohio, intending to devote himself to writing and lecturing. However, he soon became discontented without his school and after a period he bought two residences on Pennsylvania Avenue, in Denver, united them into one and opened a new sanitarium and school, having to borrow from a friend a part of the money with which to make the purchases. This probably was in 1926. This school continued until the Doctor's death, on September 1, 1940.

It was during the early years of his practice in Illinois, that Dr. Tilden began to question the use of medicine to cure illness. His extensive reading, especially of medical studies from European medical schools, and his own thinking, led him to the conclusion that there should be some way to live so as not to build disease, and in this period his thoughts on toxemia began to formulate and materially develop. From the beginning of his practice in Denver, the Doctor used no medicine but practiced his theory of clearing the body of toxic poison and then allowing nature to make the cure, teaching his patients how to live so as not to create a toxic condition and to retain a healthy body free of disease. An uncompromising realist and a strict disciplinarian, the Doctor wasted no time on those who would not relinquish degenerating habits, but to his patients and disciples he was both friend and mentor.

In 1900 he began the publication of a monthly magazine called "The Stuffed Club," which continued until 1915, when he changed the name to "The Philosophy of Health," and in 1926 the name was changed to "Health Review and Critique." His writing for his publication was almost entirely done in the early morning hours, from three until seven. The purpose of the publication was not to make money but to spread knowledge of the Doctor's teachings. In time it attained a wide circulation, not only in this country but also abroad, even in Australia, but it never produced revenue, for the Doctor refused to make it an advertising medium, as often urged to do by advertising firms. As his death revealed, after sixty-eight years of practice, the Doctor had accumulated only an exceedingly modest estate. His life was pre-eminently one of self-sacrifice and of devotion to service, searching after truth, with an indomitable will and with an intense fortitude to adhere to the truth when discovered. In his day the Doctor's thoughts received no support from the established medical profession but brought the strongest of opposition and condemnation.

Frederic N. Gilbert

DEDICATED
TO THOSE WHO ARE WILLING TO BE PRESENTED
WITH A NEW POINT OF VIEW.

The present medical opinion of venereal diseases is an infinitely greater curse to the world than will be all the diseases of mankind when they are understood and treated properly.

# Gonorrhea

—

## CHAPTER I.

—

### INTRODUCTION.

—

ENEREAL diseases are as old as the custom of wearing clothes. If mercury, potash and "606" are necessary for a cure, and if modern medical science is necessary to keep venereal disease from ruining the human race, please tell what kept the people from suffering this calamity before they had this protection.

King David cried out in the thirty-eighth psalm:

My loins are filled with a loathsome disease; and there is no soundness in my flesh. My wounds stink and are corrupt because of my foolishness.

Probably the king has reference to his people—their social life. Whether he did or not makes but little difference; what he said shows a familiarity with *venereal diseases* equaled by few public men of today. If this was the physical status of the Jewish people of that day, how did they manage to escape annihilation from syphilis? How is it that the Jewish race is as clean-blooded as any people? It is safe to say that modern medicine had nothing to do with it; it is safe to say that cleanliness, care in eating and periodic fasting had much to do with it.

### THE INFLUENCE OF CIRCUMCISION.

The Jews accomplished with circumcision, fasting and care in eating, what the Greeks brought about by baths and gymnastics. According to Renan:

The first consideration with a Greek was due care of his own person. To be sure, cleanliness and hygiene play a large part in the life of every Oriental who respects himself (be he a Jew of the old school, or a Mussulman); but the Greek training required much more. Wrestling and prescribed gymnastic exercise are repugnant to Orientals. The nudity compelled by the Greek palestra (wrestling) was shocking to them. They consider it as a leading or to vices, of which Greece, unhappily, was far too careless. In the gymnasium, circumcision was often a butt for ridicule.

The Jews and the Greeks had their own peculiar methods of prevention and cure. The Jew prevented disease by circumcision and cured it by fasting. The Greek prevented disease by baths and practicing physical culture in the nude state.

### VENEREAL DISEASES BELONG TO CLOTHES.

It is reasonable to believe that venereal diseases belong to clothes and civilization. The Greeks were perhaps more free from the so-called specific diseases than the Jews, because they bathed, went nude and exercised more than the Jews did.

The ridicule made of circumcision may have forced the Jew to keep on his clothes, and in this way caused him to be more susceptible to the disease in spite of his protective circumcision.

Either of these peoples was better off, so far as prevention and cure of venereal disease are concerned, than we are today. No doubt these great people "builded better than they knew;" but we do not build as well as we know. We have all of past history to draw from, yet we refuse to be taught by the experience of the past. Our treatment of diseases is a disgrace to our age, and our prevention, except in the line of sanitation, is an insult to intelligence.

## VENEREAL DISEASES AND THE SOLDIER.

The American soldier suffered more from venereal diseases, vaccination and smallpox in the Philippine Islands than from all other diseases. The natives had religion shot into them, and clothes shot onto them; air and sun were kept from their bodies, and they were made to understand that they must not *expose their bodies* by going into the water, as had been their habit; they were taught modesty before cleanliness—and the result has become history.

· We learn from history that venereal diseases belong to civilization. The disease came to America with the white man, and just how and when it landed once gave mental exercise to the profession. Just how it landed was discovered, but time refuted the alleged discovery.

John Hunter came dangerously near the truth *when he discovered* that gonorrhea and syphilis were one, but as he did not discover that all decomposition—that the poison peculiar to all ulcerations—is one and the same thing, his discovery has been ignored by the profession and passed as one of the mistakes of a great man.

When a country is civilized—given clothes and modesty— the *diseases that primitive habits prevented and cured* are made virulent.

Civilizing education is always in line for building the most virulent type of venereal disease: and how about wounds of any kind? Isn't such education the very best for converting every wound and disease into a virulent type?

## WOUND AND VENEREAL TREATMENT.

The treatment that will cure a wound will cure gonorrhea and syphilis; a treatment that will cause a wound to take on infection will do the same for a venereal disease.

The curse of civilization is that it comes before natural, mental protection, and immunization from disease, are understood.

Cause and effect must be the same today that they have ever been; then possibilities for disease are the same and will remain the same. The aboriginal man died from an infected wound, the same as his civilized descendants. His descendants, however, died oftener; for they *learned how to dress and keep their wounds from being exposed* to the sun and air. Only just now a few have learned that wounds must be drained—that an open, exposed wound is less liable to take on infection than one closed up. This lesson is not half learned; for deaths from septic infection are of daily occurrence among the patients of our best physicians and in our most perfected hospitals. Only a short time ago diphtheria broke out in Johns Hopkins Hospital. The Lord save us!

The lower down in the scale of civilization we go, the more severe are the types of all diseases that take on septic infection. The so-called infectious and contagious diseases are found in their worst types among those who know enough to hide their nakedness, but who have no conception of what cleanliness is or what it is for. Ignorance unclothed is far better off than when clothed. The fig leaf was the beginning of man's undoing. So long as modesty and morality must be defined in terms of ignorance, just so long will humanity suffer with the diseases peculiar to filth.

We are told today that syphilis is a disease caused by a germ—the spirocheta pallida. This will be discussed to a finish by my former assistant. Dr. R. L. Alsaker; indeed, there is no need of my saying more than to make this reference. I shall have something to say, however, on the nature of syphilis that has not been said before, that I know of, and which, of course, I think worth saying. See page 71.

## ORIGIN OF DISEASE.

At present the theory that disease originates from exogenous causes is universally received, and dissenting opinions are ignored —in fact, treated much as if they were not.

Bigotry and intolerance are characteristic of a class of scientists who discover, announce their discoveries to their scientific congress, the membership of which is composed of men like themselves, and then vote the acceptance of their discoveries. If there are opponents, they will be given to understand that they are in the kindergarten.

They will be referred to in the manner of the following, which I quote from an opening speech of Louis Pasteur to the congress of scientists about 1880:

Gentlemen: Your congress meetings are the place for the discussion of the great problems of medicine; they serve also to point out the great landmarks of the future. Three years ago, on the eve of the London congress, the doctrine of micro-organisms, the ætiological cause of transmissible maladies, was still the subject of sharp criticisms. Certain refractory minds continued to uphold the idea that "disease is in us, from us, by us."

It was expected that the decided supporters of the theory of the spontaneity of disease would make a bold stand in London; but no opposition was made to the doctrine of "exteriority," or external causes, the first cause of contagious diseases, and those questions were not discussed at all.

It was there seen, once again, that when all is ready for the final triumph of truth, the united conscience of a great assembly feels it instinctively and recognizes it.

There is confidence in those words; they have the ring of a victor, and he and those who were with him in this matter had won out. Over whom? Over those who believed in spontaneous generation. Both sides *assumed* that disease came from germs. Had they proven their assumption? No! Nor were they in position to prove it, for *they were not physicians;* and I want to impress it on the memory of every reader that any conscientious, busy country physician is entitled to more respect, when it comes to telling what the cause of disease is, than a dozen of such scientists as Mr. Pasteur.

### DRUGS MASK SYMPTOMS

The physician has kept himself bewildered by the use of drugs; disease being almost immediately masked by the drugs which he has given for their *supposed remedial* influence.

Masking symptoms with drugs has put such a handicap on the profession that its opinions have become a joke, and so little has the best physician known about cause that he really could have no opinion; hence, the scientist has undertaken to put in a foundation of fact by assuming that germs cause disease, and the doctor has not been in position to do more than accept; for, if he did not believe it, he was not in position to dispute it. This is why the scientist is so arbitrary and conceited about his relationship to the profession. He really assumes to be the whole thing—which he is from the present status of the profession.

A doctor who has not treated a venereal disease without drugs knows nothing about an uncomplicated disease; hence, if there are such who will presume to criticise my treatment, he can be set down as a bigoted ass who has a lot to learn.

## THREE DAYS CURES.

There is a lot of popular ignorance on the subject of gonorrhea. The impression is prevalent that the disease can be cured in three days, and there are people who declare they, or people they have known, have been cured in a few days. This is a falsehood that causes much trouble; for those who believe it are unwilling to submit to rational treatment, and when by their own foolishness they bring upon themselves all sorts of complications, and suffer for months or even years, they charge their misfortunes to the *fool doctor*, who should have cured them the first week. Too often this opinion is made patent by ignorant or dishonest physicians who are so short-sighted as to attempt to build a reputation by tearing down the reputation of others. All such lay ignorance has its origin in the profession—among unscrupulous physicians. While on this subject I cannot do better than quote from a well-known authority on the moral aspect of the disease:

## THE MORAL STATUS.

The treatment of urethritis is accompanied by moral difficulties not experienced to the same extent in connection with any other malady. When a man gets urethritis he rarely feels willing to acknowledge that it is largely, perhaps wholly, his own fault; and it is not customary to see him stand up and take his punishment like a man. He generally accuses his partner of all the blame for his misfortune, although she, indeed, may have no contagious disease; he feels ashamed of himself, tries to sneak out of his troubles, and demands of his physician anything and everything, asserting that he positively must be cured in a few days. He will nearly always demand, with impatience, how long it will be before he will be well, and he calls for violent measures in order that the course of the disease may be cut short. If he is not satisfied on these points, and promised a speedy cure, he refers to some friend, or perhaps to a number of friends, who laugh at gonorrhea, and tell him that they constantly get it and cure it for themselves in a few days with some favorite prescription; and it is

by the standard of this misinformation from friends that the result of the physician's efforts is often judged.

In syphilis the patient is far more frightened than when he has gonorrhea,
but he never disturbs the physician by asking for a cure within a few days.
The popular idea about syphilis is that it lasts forever, and the patient with
this disease asks his physician not to cure him promptly, but whether he ever
can get the poison thoroughly out of his "system," as he puts it.

If, therefore, the surgeon allows himself to be browbeaten by the ignorance of his patient, he has to commence the treatment of urethritis—a very
obstinate disease—under most disadvantageous auspices; and the patient is apt
in the end to be dissatisfied with the result, no matter how creditable that result
may really be. To be just to himself, the surgeon must start as master of the
field, if he hopes for any comfort; and the only way to do this with a foolish
young man suffering from his first attack, or with an anxious husband who
expects his wife to return home in ten days, is to have a perfect understanding
at the very commencement of treatment

The patient should be informed that gonorrhea, badly managed is a.
serious a matter, in many cases, as syphilis; that gonorrhea probably kills more
patients than syphilis does, through its ultimate effect, by means of stricture of
the urethra, upon the bladder and the kidneys. If the patient's associates find
gonorrhea to be so light a matter, it is well to refer him back to them for treatment. The surgeon should absolutely refuse in any case to give a promise of
cure in any given time. He cannot give such an assurance honestly, and if he
happens to hit right with his guess in the case of one patient, that patient will
injure his reputation greatly; for he will boast among his companions of a
prompt cure within a certain promised number of days, and his friends will
come with their gonorrheas and denounce the physician as incompetent. No
man can positively assert at the start whether a given urethral inflammation just
commencing at the pouting orifice of a healthy urethra is to be a severe case or
not, or whether it will yield a prompt response to remedies.

If a man has already had several attacks of gonorrhea, and his present
attack comes on without any œdematous swelling of the meatus urinarius, the
chances are that the attack will be a mild one. If the case is one of first
attack, and there has been not more than forty-eight hours' incubation, the
chances also are that the inflammation will not be violent. If there has been no

sexual intercourse at all to occasion the new outbreak, then, although the course of the malady may be slow and its duration protracted, the symptoms are not apt to run high.

In any case, so far as making a prognosis is concerned, it is proper to say to the patient that he has a disorder which is perfectly curable by gentle treatment, but which often fails to get well if harsh measures are used; that the symptoms require intelligent management, according to their intensity; that it is safer and surer in the end to make haste slowly, and that all will be done by treatment that can be effected by drugs.

Under such an understanding, the surgeon's hands are free, and the patient's mind at rest, because he (the patient), under the circumstances, will either seek treatment elsewhere, or he will yield himself up to his physician, and follow his instructions with willing confidence. Then, if the case turns out to be a mild one, and gets well in a fortnight, the patient is delighted and appreciative. If it drags itself along for two or three months, he is regretful, but satisfied.

The Abortive Treatment of Gonorrhea should not be attempted. It is accompanied by considerable danger, and is absolutely uncertain. Those cases which get well under its use are cases of urethritis which doubtless would have recovered promptly under mild treatment. When it does not cure, it greatly increases the grade of intensity of the inflammation, and leads with much certainty to stricture ultimately, and immediately in many cases to complications on the side of the bladder and testicle, not devoid of danger to important functions. As a general rule, it will be found that those who have most faith in the value of the abortive treatment are those who have not tried it at all, or medical men and young practitioners who have not had much experience with the disease. After a few disastrous failures the practice is generally abandoned. The few authorities in high position who advocate the abortive treatment are becoming yearly more oracular in their utterances, more reserved in promising any certain effect from the use of harsh injections very early in the course of a gonorrhea. I do not assert that abortive treatment does not sometimes seem to cut short any attack of urethral inflammation, but I certainly maintain that no man can assert that it will always do so, no matter how it is used; and I believe that the damage it does in the cases in which it fails far outbalances the alleged good it accomplishes in cases of apparent success. I doubt greatly whether a true, virulent gonorrhea can be aborted by the use of strong astringent injections at the start.

The treatment of urethritis which aims at an intelligent management of th_ symptoms according to their intensity, once adopted, is not likely to be given up for any other plan, because the results are in the main so satisfactory. This treatment is hygienic and medicinal.

### HYGIENIC TREATMENT OF URETHRITIS.

Absolute regularity of life should be enjoined in all cases from the start; anything l.ke irregularity is detrimental. The patient should rest as much as pos-ible, lying down rather than sitting or walking. He should, indeed, avoid exercise at first, and keep as far as possible in a uniform temperature. Regularity should be practiced in sleeping and in eating, and particular attention should be bestowed upon the function of the intestines.

The amount of food taken at the beginning of an attack should be moderate, its quality bland and unstimulating, its nature light and varied. If the patient be debilitated, on the other hand, plenty of meat should be allowed, the full ordinary amount of food should be taken, and in some cases even a little red wine from the very beginning. Milk is an excellent article of diet in all cases. Where it cannot be promptly digested, the work of the stomach may be made easier by adding salt to the milk; and a laxative, such as a dinner pill, may be given at night; or a little compound liquorice powder, or, if the patient prefers, some bitter sulphate of soda-water in the morning

Among the articles of food to be avoided in all acute cases (excepting those coming on in decidedly debilitated subjects, when intelligent exceptions must be made) are pastry, gravies, fried fats, and greasy articles of food; all rich made-dishes and indigestible substances, all condiments of every description, excepting the mildest form. Salt, however, is not objectionable, pickles and acids usually are. Asparagus is harmful to some patients.

Among the drinks to be avoided are strong coffee and tea; chocolate in any form, since this beverage stimulates the sexual appetite; all wines and liquors of any description, particularly the fermented wines and malt liquors.

Soda-water, root-beer and Vichy water may be used as beverages with decided advantage, and the more water that can be taken between meals the better, particularly rain-water, which is very bland to the stomach and a mild diuretic.   It is always well for patients to take a full glass of water upon retiring, so that the morning urine may be less dense than would otherwise be the case.

Smoking is not objectionable.

The mind should be kept absolutely free from impure thoughts during the whole of the attack, and no sexual excitement permitted for a moment.   The penis should be handled as little as possible.

The latter precaution must be strictly enforced, for two reasons:  In the first place, the constant pulling of the urethra, in order to see how much pus it contains and what its quality may be, is very irritating to the inflamed mucous membrane of the canal.   In the second place, fingering the urethra exposes the eyes of the patient to inadvertent inoculation.   The caution of extreme cleanliness and avoidance of the contact of any pus from the urethra with the conjunctiva should be very forcibly given to each patient, and frequently repeated and insisted upon.

As a final hygienic precaution it is well for the patient to carry his testicles in a suspensory bandage, since the tendency to epididymitis is in this way decidedly lessened.

All the hygienic precautions alluded to should be held in force during the whole course of an urethral discharge, and for a considerable period after its apparent cessation (a week or ten days) through fear of a relapse.

I quote the above from Professor E. L. Keyes' work on "Venereal Diseases," published in 1880.   Notwithstanding the book was written thirty years ago, I doubt if anyone has said anything better on the moral aspect of this subject than the few paragraphs quoted above; they have the ring of a man who was master of the situation—who knew the need of having the confidence and necessarily the full control of his patient.

## PHYSICIANS MUST CONTROL PATIENTS.

It is necessary for a physician to have absolute control of every patient, and especially is this true of those who are being treated for sexual diseases; for disturbances of the sexual organs are peculiarly demoralizing, and the venereal subjects must be controlled. Professional men of a negative type will not be successful in treating gonorrhea.

A thorough understanding at the beginning of the treatment is necessary. The patient must be given to understand that more depends upon himself in getting well quickly than on the doctor. The doctor should give the patient to understand that he, the doctor, cannot cure *any disease;* that nature does the curing when there is any curing done; that all that he can do, or can honestly pretend to do, is to teach the patient how to care for himself so that nature will not be hindered in her reparative work. Explain that as complications are brought about by needless neglect on the part of the patient, and that when the disease is prolonged it comes from a reinfection of himself from neglect in carrying out instructions.

## PAY IN ADVANCE.

The physician should take his pay in advance, and then give the patient to understand that the quicker the cure the more advantage to both. If the fee is taken in advance, the patient will not be so inclined to become restless and want to run to some doctor, of whom a friend has *just* told him, who promises to cure in three days. All patients follow instructions better when made to pay in advance; for they know that they must attend to business if they can hope to get their money's worth. If a patient does not pay in advance, he can afford (many are ignorant enough to believe) to prolong his disease; for if he does not get well, he will not feel under any moral responsibility to pay the doctor: *if the doctor does not cure him, of course he does not owe him anything.*

It is proper to charge by the month and take the pay monthly in advance, and then explain to the patient that he can get well in from two to four weeks, and that a second month's treatment will not be necessary unless he fails to follow instructions, which being his fault, he should be the only one to suffer. Doctors are imposed upon by this class of patients; they blame them for not curing them, when it is impossible; for they break all instructions.

Doctors are largely to blame for the bad treatment they get; *it is a doctor's business to control his patient, and to lodge* the responsibility of a lingering disease where it belongs.

Of course, the conventional treatment is uncertain, and in *too* many instances is really the cause of prolongation and complications; but with the treatment I shall teach, the doctor can be master of the situation, and speak confidently about the cure; and demand that instructions be followed; and, if the patient fails to get well as predicted, the doctor can declare, confidently and authoritatively, that the reason he is not doing well, if he is not, is because he has not followed instructions.

It is a real pleasure to treat venereal diseases when the physician is sure of his treatment; but there is no greater nightmare than to undertake to cure these diseases with the element of uncertainty so pronounced as it is with the best treatment advanced by the profession today.

I hope every physician who reads this book will proceed to carry out my plan in every detail, and not fail to prepare the minds of his patients in advance by explaining to them how necessary it is that they do everything just as instructed, and if they do they will have a comfortable sickness, and both doctor and patient will be delighted.

## CHAPTER II.

### THE UNITY OF INFECTION.

 HOLD to the idea that all poisoning, other than chemical, is from decomposition, and is one and the same thing. Is this more inconceivable than the fact that coal and diamond are the same; that water—*aqua pura*—is the same as peroxide of hydrogen; that Pius IX and Alexander VI were both popes; that Cæsar Borgia and Richelieu were cardinals? As to the reason why I select men, or different types of minds, I wish to refer to an object that can be accepted as a single substance—or element, if you please—which has an infinite variety of expressions. Is there anything to exceed mind? Any of the so-called elements has an infinite variety of expressions.

We know that water and peroxide are not alike; they are wholly unlike in every way; yet they are made different by simply adding an atom more of oxygen.

When the human organism is normal, the blood and fluids of the body are slightly alkaline. The fluid in the sheaths of the nerves is alkaline; when this fluid loses its alkalinity the nerves go wrong. A slight deviation from the normal brings nervous symptoms, and the symptoms change as the fluids change, growing worse as the alkalinity gives way to acidity. As acidity develops, the secretions and excretions so affected show a change in the functions of the organs that furnish them; and if this state continues long, we may expect organic change, and the functions of the entire body will change to correspond. Emotionally, for instance, the disposition will change from a sweet, hopeful, sunny nature to a fault-finding, suspicious, grouchy nature; and there must be a physical change to correspond.

### AN ACID STATE.

The simplest change, when there is a decrease in alkalinity, is the development of warts and other simple skin blemishes; when the vaginal secretions become quite acid, I have seen very great numbers of venereal warts spring up on the vulva. One negress, a patient of mine twenty-six years ago, had these warts developed to the size of two large fists.

These growths are the result of a slight change in the secretions, plus germs. Why do not the germs attack the parts when normal? They probably do, but a normal state renders their attacks impotent for harm. In all probability all the germs that infest the body are properly nourished when the body is normal, and only become alienated when their normal food is changed; then their nature changes and they become enemies.

### THE INFLUENCE OF MERCURY.

When mercury is given under such circumstances, what influence does it have? It becomes a rank poison, producing inflammation and ulceration; and if its administration be continued, instead of the surface of the body being attacked, the deep structures become involved through infection of the lymphatic glands.

What is it that affects the glands? Mercury? No, septic absorption. Where does septic absorption come from, if the ulceration is caused by mercury? From the same source as when it comes from a gunshot wound; a compound, complicated fracture, retention of secretions after childbirth; a wound by a rusty nail, or the bite of a dog. All these wounds, if not drained and kept free from the accumulating decomposing debris, will become infected, and septic absorption will be stopped by the lymphatic glands; for they act as sentinels, ready to arrest invaders. However, if the absorption of infection continues, the glands will not only fail to hold back the infection, but they will suppurate and become a source of secondary infection.

When the fluids of the body are normal in their chemistry, it can be said that the body has normal resistance; but when the energy is used up by excess in one or more lines, enervation is brought on. This means weakened function, with necessarily a retention of waste products. Then digestion suffers: for if the *mill-ends*, so to speak, are retained, the intake must be cut down, or there will be faulty digestion added to faulty elimination, and before we are aware of it we have a patient seriously autotoxemic. This is the acid state referred to above, and it should be known that while in this state drugs will have a varying action. The physician will say: "Sometimes I get a kindly action and sometimes I do not; the drug does not have a uniform action. Food sometimes acts nicely and again it does not." The reason for these variations must be understood, or the medical man will always be groping in the dark.

If drugs and food vary so much in their action—or, to put it in another way, if the reaction of the body on food and drugs is so great—what is to prevent a great variety of reactions when poisoned by the ordinary disease-producing agents?

## WHY ONE IS POISONED AND ANOTHER IS NOT.

An individual with normal secretions handles the rhus tox. vine with impunity, while one with an acid reaction suffers poisoning; and the degree of poisoning will be in keeping with his resistance—the greater his acidity, the less resistance.

If we turn to erysipelas, we have a poisoning resembling rhus tox., the difference being in the nature of the infection. The erysipelas poisoning is of a septic character; the animal decomposition may be developed within the patient's digestive system, or the poison may be conveyed from without. The physician who handles the case and is careless may convey infection to his obstetric patient; yet, if she is not in this peculiarly susceptible state, he is not liable to infect her, for she is possessed of neutralizing and resisting power. If he infects her, what will her disease be? Erysipelas? Not what we call erysipelas; she will have puerperal fever. Suppose the doctor continues to be careless and conveys the infection of erysipelas to a surgical case—one in which the drainage is imperfect; this patient will develop septicemia, if he is in a receptive state, but if he is not, his wound cannot be made to take on infection unless septic material is forced into the blood by being bound on the wound. If this same doctor should use instruments in treating a case of gonorrhea, and then, without proper cleaning, use them on his puerperal woman, what would result? If she were not normal, she would be thrown into puerperal septicemia. Or if the doctor should forget and use a finger recently injured in examining a neglected gonorrhea or syphilis, or thoughtlessly put the finger into a diphtheritic throat or ulcerating wound, or get the discharge from a glandered horse into the wound, what would he develop, if he developed anything? "Blood poisoning." But what would be

the nature of the blood poisoning? Septicemia! The disease
would not be different from an auto-generated septicemia—it would
be the same as develops from an undrained and an improperly
dressed wound.

My object in going over all this is to show the interchangeableness of the so-called specific infections.   If the reader would
have my meaning, think of light, heat, electricity, etc., and of the
peculiar interchangeableness of their natures.   The thought I wish
to convey is that septic poisoning is capable of appearing as puerperal fever, erysipelas, typhoid fever, bubonic plague, diphtheria,
scarlet fever, wound infection; indeed, all blood poisonings, including gonorrhea and syphilis.

# CHAPTER III.

## Gonorrhea.

EFORE going into the subject of gonorrhea proper, I wish to spend a little time in going over the theory of specific infection; for on this the prevailing treatment rests, and if I am to succeed in winning adherents to my plan of treatment, it is necessary for me to show a good reason for not believing that God created the gonococcus just to punish man for his misdeeds.

### SIMPLE AND SPECIFIC INFLAMMATION.

The difference, I assume, between a simple and a specific urethritis is the same as between a simple and a septic inflammation of any other part of the body. I recognize sepsis as the only infecting agent in all so-called specific diseases. The toxic element in all diseases is sepsis. I assume that all secretions, excretions and exudations are non-toxic until they are forced to become toxic by decomposition, and that all germs are innocent until their habitat has become toxic from putrefaction.

Will the reader please do himself the justice, and me the honor, of reading my argument to the end before passing adversely on what I have to say? Then, if he is not convinced, he has no right to condemn my theory and treatment until he has tried it out in a few cases, using great care to carry out my instructions to the letter.

When an inflammation is not given the rest, physiological and otherwise, necessary, and drainage is imperfect or inhibited entirely, the exudation takes on decomposition, after which local or general infection takes place.

The swelling of the mucous membrane, and the sensitiveness and soreness of the organ, involved in an inflammatory process, interfere with its mechanism, prevent the rapid removal of the inflammatory exudates, and this retention favors putrefaction and auto-infection. This is especially true of inflammations of narrow canals and tubes. The only reason a fatal infection does not take place is because the obstruction is not complete.

In penetrating wounds, if the drainage is imperfect, there will be delay in healing; if the obstruction is sufficient to allow decomposition to take place in the exudates, yet not complete, the infection will be local; but when the obstruction is complete, general infection will follow so rapidly that twenty-four hours will often place the patient beyond recovery.

Is there any difference in the specific inflammations of the different organs of the body? Modern medical science declares that there is, and that a specific germ marks the difference—that without the germ the specific disease cannot be developed.

Every part of the body is subject to its special types of disease. The lungs are subject to pneumonia, bronchitis, pleurisy and tuberculosis. Typhoid fever is said to take its origin in the bowels, from infection, along with appendicitis, typhlitis and colitis. When meningitis is mentioned, we think of the membranes of the brain and spinal cord; carditis, inflammation of the heart; metritis, inflammation of the womb. And so I might go on and bring in review every organ of the body; but I have mentioned enough for

my purpose. Every organ or tissue of the body stamps with individuality its diseases; yet inflammation is the same in whatever
tissue found, and, if great enough, it will be accompanied with
systemic sympathy, which is known as fever—increased temperature—and general disturbance of nutrition.

Inflammation ends in resolution or suppuration. If nutrition
is impaired and there is much so-called blood or glandular derangement, local inflammations are more inclined to ulcerate and
suppurate.

Local inflammations caused by injury get well quickly or not,
depending upon the general health of the one injured and aseptic
treatment. If there has been a cutting or tearing of the flesh, healing will be uninterrupted, provided the injured part is kept clean
and the blood normal; but if drainage is imperfect, the exudation
will take on a septic change, and, being held on the granulating
surface, absorption is forced, following which systemic infection
takes place, and then we have septicemia—sometimes called trau-
matic or surgical fever.

That the reader may know the relationship of all septic or
specific fevers, I will say that there appears to be no difference in
the effect of an infection, whether it be absorbed from an infected
wound coming from an injury, an ulcer in typhoid, a wound of
the womb or soft parts caused by childbirth or abortion, or the discharge from a urethra in clap or from an ulcerating bubo, except in
degree, and the degree depends upon the amount of septic material
absorbed.

### SPECIAL GERMS.

It is taught that there are special germs distinguishing all diseases. However this may be primarily, when systemic infection

occurs, the constitutional effect is the same; and I assume that all special inflammations, when pushed to the stage where septic absorption takes place, end in the same way and from the same cause.

Septic infection is virulent in proportion to the amount absorbed. If the ulcerating surface is large in typhoid fever, and the accumulation of septic material in the intestine great, enough will be absorbed to overwhelm the patient, and death will follow. If the position of the womb is such that drainage cannot take place, the normal discharge will be pent up and become putrescent, immediately following which there will be symptoms of septicemia, and if not recognized and drainage established, death will often follow within two days. If drainage is imperfect, the discharge may not be held long enough for virulent putrefaction to take place in it; yet enough degenerative change takes place to set up a local infection, following which there will be chronic inflammation and suppuration of different parts of the generative organs and adjacent tissues. This explains why all patients do not die when septically infected. Of course, the patient's general health will have something to do with the intensity of the disease; however, when a putrescent material is pent up in the womb, or in a wound, it will kill the strongest woman or man as quickly as it will kill the weakest.

Perhaps the readers will be curious by this time to know the relevancy of all this to the subject of gonorrhea. It is this: All discharges from wounds and inflamed mucous surfaces are peculiar to the organs affected, but when these discharges are pent up and forced to take on putrefaction, the poisoning is that of septicemia, be it from an injury, from clap, syphilis, or pulmonary tuberculosis; and when patients suffering with typhoid fever, a wound, abortion, tuberculosis, syphilis or gonorrhea die from infection, they die from septicemia.

What causes the fever in tuberculosis? Septic absorption. In gonorrhea and syphilis, what causes the complications, such as fever and glandular inflammation (buboes)? Septic infection. Why is the infection confined locally? Why does it not kill as wound infection, typhoid fever and puerperal septicemia? All wound infections, typhoid and puerperal fevers do not end in death. Clap and syphilis would prove fatal if the discharges from the urethra or chancre were pent up until sufficiently putrefied, and then absorbed into the blood. The true cause of death, however would be septic—septicemia. If venereal diseases could be treated properly from the start, there would not be enough infective material absorbed to cause much inconvenience.

## CHAPTER IV.

### VENEREAL DISEASES ARE SKIN DISEASES.

I HAVE become convinced, after years of observation, that venereal diseases are, strictly speaking, skin diseases, and will remain skin diseases until recovery takes place, unless forced by maltreatment to become constitutional. There is no more reason for recognizing a gonorrhea or a chancre as a blood disease than there is for believing a simple wound or a vaccination blood disease, until by maltreatment these latter wounds to the skin are forced to take on enough ulceration to develop septic poisoning.

I know this is rank heresy, but I am forced to believe it from experience.

It will be asked: How do you account for certain specific symptoms that develop months, and sometimes years, after the primary chancre has been cured? In each and every subject so afflicted there are the habits of the sensualist and dissolute, and their organisms have also been abused by drugs enough to account for every symptom. Besides, how often are physicians forced to account for these symptoms by assuming that patients have been infected in some unaccountable way?

From my standpoint, all is accounted for; from the viewpoint of present medical belief, improbable assumption is worked overtime.

Again: "How about the Wasserman test?" My answer is: How about it? Isn't it a fact that it sometimes works and again it does not? Then I will ask: Why is it that, in spite of all specific cures, in reality no cures are made? Proof of this is found in the fact that when a patient is once a syphilitic he is always a syphilitic. If not, why is he catechised on the subject, and treated for syphilis by the best physicians as long as he lives?

When the profession is once awakened to the truth on this subject, venereal disease will cease to be the nemesis that now stalks on the heels of thousands of good men who have repented in sack-cloth and ashes before a Jehovah more deaf, relentless and intolerant than the one built by the Jewish bigots of old.

The present medical opinion of venereal diseases is an infinitely greater curse to the world than will be all the diseases of mankind when they are understood and treated properly.

Gonococci are characteristic of purulent urethritis; the diphtheritic germ is peculiar to ulcerative tonsilitis; the bacillus of tuberculosis is found in ulcerative lung and pleural diseases. When systemic infection takes place, these germs are carried into the general system through absorption from their special habitat.

Without ulceration these germs do not take on specificity.

We have authority for the statement that tuberculosis has been known to exist for six to eighteen months before the germ could be found. I have known of a few cases of abscess of the liver, discharging through the bronchial tubes, diagnosed pulmonary tuberculosis because of the presence of the tuberculosis germs in the pus expectorated.

Empyema (pus in the pleura) that discharges through the lungs is frequently diagnosed tuberculosis because the germs are found in the expectorated pus.   And other germs are found, or could be found if looked for.   Then, why not hold them responsible for creating the disease?

The difference between a simple inflammation and a septic inflammation is that simple inflammation is started by an injury or non-toxic irritation, and if the cause is removed, recovery will take place very quickly; but if the cause is continued and cleanliness neglected, thickening of the mucous membrane and ulceration will be brought on.   Then, if the exudation cannot pass away freely, decomposition takes place, with local infection and a possibility of systemic septicemia.

A specific infection is a septic infection.   Contact is had with discharges that are putrescent.   If drainage is perfect and the discharge washed away—positive cleanliness practiced—the primary infection will end in five to ten days; but if drainage and cleanliness are neglected, reinfection will occur so often that death from general septic infection is a remote possibility.   It is only when skin infection becomes blood infection that life is menaced.

When drainage is perfect, primary infections end shortly after the exciting cause subsides; but when drainage is imperfect, decomposition of the exudate becomes an independent cause lighting up fresh infections.

Gonorrhea, next to syphilis, is the most important venereal disease, and, like syphilis, is said to be a "peril to civilization," a "terrible scourge."

My experience forces me to believe that, if these strong statements are true, the cause lies in the treatment.

When a physician declares that venereal disease is a "terrible scourge," he is unconsciously advertising his own unfavorable experience, and then drawing on his imagination about the experience of others, which, *of course, must be worse than his.* In this way such writers find material for their exaggerations.

There is no question but that there are people who are ruined in mind and body from the supposed ravages of venereal diseases; when the truth is that the treatment has caused most of their discomfort.

When I say that the modern medical treatment of venereal diseases is infinitely more to be dreaded than the disease, I am not taken seriously. The world has become so accustomed to hyperbole that my denunciation of the present popular education on syphilis—the books for popular reading, and plays such as "Damaged Goods"—is looked upon as hysteria or hypocrisy. We appear to be suffering from a wave of credulity, on such subjects as the cause and treatment of diseases generally, that would do credit to a world of infants or idiots.

Look at the reports on salvarsan and neosalvarsan for the past winter (1913-14): deaths, injuries to eyes, and damaged health galore are reported from private, as well as hospital, practice. At the moment of this writing a grand jury is trying to solve the reason for seven deaths that have taken place in a Los Angeles hospital within twenty-four hours after the victims were given neosalvarsan hypodermically. And a special cable of March 14, 1914, to the *Chicago Tribune* declares:

The attacks on Dr. Ehrlich and his specific salvarsan in German medical circles are more aggressive than those which were made a year or two ago on Dr. Friedmann and his turtle serum.

The whole question soon will be aired in the courts in a suit for libel against an editor of one of the leading papers of Frankfort. The editor made a charge in his paper against the city authorities and the physicians of the city hospital of Frankfort. He said the hospital physicians had applied salvarsan to an unfortunate woman against her will and despite her resistance. This editor also charged that the hospital doctors are using the patients as "experimental rabbits," and offered to bring evidence that at least fifteen deaths, and any number of cases of blindness and paralysis, had resulted from the use of salvarsan. As could be expected, the hospital physicians made a general denial of what the paper stated, and brought an action for libel against the editor. It is the general belief, however, that the newspaper man will have no difficulty in proving his charges.

Drinking-cups have been removed from trains and public places; yet the venereal-saturated cooks, bakers, bar and soda-fountain tenders, dish-washers, candy-makers, dairy milkers, bottle-washers, barbers, hair-dressers, vegetable-vendors, stamp- and money-handlers and money itself, and, neither last nor least, surgical and dental instruments, continue to hand out the real article, with no apologies to the pure-food laws. The public drinking-cup is a bagatelle when compared with the soda fountain, to say nothing about the dishes in public eating-houses.

If venereal diseases could be transmitted by drinking-cups or by the contamination imparted to inanimate objects by labor employes, the world would have been depopulated long ago.

### INFECTION BY CONTACT.

There is little danger of infection except by contact of an abraded surface with the virus of contagion. When nerve energy is at par and resistance great, infection will have to be equivalent to inoculation—the virus must be rubbed in.

# CHAPTER V.

---

## SYMPTOMS.

---

ONORRHEA is an inflammation of the urethra, accompanied by a discharge of creamy consistency, of more or less thickness, and of a yellowish color. The mouth of the urethra becomes red and pouting within a day or two after the discharge is established, and if the victim is troubled with a highly acid urine, the redness and pouting increase, with rawness or an excoriation of the mucous membrane. When this occurs, the patient suffers greatly while passing urine and is getting dangerously near systemic infection.

### IMPORTANCE OF FASTING.

Unless those who are decidedly autotoxemic are fasted or placed upon a very light diet, and taught how to be scrupulously cleanly, the urethral inflammation will become so intense that sloughing will take place, allowing the deeper tissues to become involved; which means that septic infection of the blood is starting up.

The foreskin often becomes edematous—swollen to resemble a bladder of water. When this infiltration is great, it is almost impossible to push it back, and it makes a very disagreeable complication, interfering greatly with cleanliness. Unless the accumulation under the swollen foreskin is thoroughly washed out by irrigation with a fountain syringe, decomposition of secretions or exudates takes place, causing ulceration of the foreskin and absorption or the septic material, after which the glands in the groin become involved in a septic inflammation and ulceration. Inflamed inguinal glands are called buboes (sometimes vulgarly called "bluebore").

At this stage inflammation of the bladder or prostate, or both, may develop. Then urination will become frequent, with inability to hold the urine. In severe cases it will be passed as often as every fifteen minutes. So frequently is it necessary to void urine, and in such small amounts, that the unfortunate victim is compelled to wear a folded towel to catch the discharge, which would be expelled before he could have time to get to the most convenient urinal; for the desire is so great that it brings on spasmodic contractions of the bladder, which place the act beyond the control of the will.

*Orchitis.*—This is the stage where orchitis—inflammation of the testicles—occurs; a complication that causes the patient to suffer hell, if he has not already suffered it. The sequels of orchitis are rheumatism, and not infrequently sterility and suicidal mania.

# CHAPTER VI.

## THE TREATMENT OF GONORRHEA.

THE treatment for gonorrhea is so simple that many will hesitate and be afraid to adopt it. The profession and the people cannot give up the idea that a successful treatment must be *scientific*, difficult, and hard to understand and carry out.

When humanity evolves enough common sense to realize that cures are beyond doctors and healers, that nature does all the healing that can be done, and that all suffering is caused by nature's effort at conservation, then there will be an opportunity for people to get well in the shortest possible time, and at the least expenditure of nerve energy from unnecessary and foolish treatment.

When doctors declare that venereal diseases require a specific treatment, do not take what they say too seriously; for they do not know—they have not tried. The doctor who believes that venereal diseases cannot be cured without drugs simply advertises himself as unwise—a man willing to dispute without investigation. I dispute that drugs can cure anything, and I do so after *having successfully used them* for twenty-five years.

When I am consulted by a gonorrheal subject, I prescribe a light diet, and frequent local hot baths followed by cold water. Place the penis in hot water—as hot as can be borne—for five or ten minutes; then follow with a cold-water sponging. It is well to use soap with the hot water.  Great care must be given to the fore-skin; it must be pulled back and thoroughly washed inside and out. When the symptoms are active and there is much discomfort in uri-nating, the baths should be taken every three hours, or at least three times a day.

### DRESSING FOR GONORRHEA.

A towel should be worn to catch the discharge.  The best manner of adjusting the towel is as follows:  Tie or pin a belt of muslin, two inches wide (or a cord will do), around the body, either at the waist or lower if desired.   It should be pinned or tied snug enough to prevent it from slipping down over the hips.   Then take an ordinary hand towel and slip one end under the belt, bring-ing it up enough above the belt to leave the lower end long enough to come down to the lower third of the thighs; then pin the towel, full width, to the belt or cord.   It should be long enough to protect all the clothing from being soiled by the discharge.   This will save the victim the humiliation of advertising his disease to the launderer or laundress.   No one with proper self-respect, or possessed of decent consideration for others, will send linen to the laundry soiled with gonorrheal or any other discharge.   By adjusting the towel correctly it can be gathered about the genitals so as to keep all the discharge on the towel.

The advantage in wearing this dressing is that the penis is not constricted, but allowed perfect freedom, so that the drainage from the urethra can be complete; for as fast as the discharge is secreted it passes out on the towel.   When the discharge is great, at least three towels should be used each twenty-four hours; for the penis must not be allowed to rest against a discharge-saturated dressing. At every urination—which will not be more frequent than every

three hours—if possible, wash the glans penis and foreskin, and
apply a little white vaseline to the mouth of the urethra before
returning the organ behind the dressing, and always to a clean part
of it.    Absolute cleanliness, with free drainage, will bring a rapid
cure without a single complication, and perfect comfort will be
secured after the first few days to a week.    Eating should be light:
if there is much pain in urinating, a pint of clabber-milk three times
a day is quite enough food. . When comfortable, the eating may be
light—of any food except potatoes and meat.    Positively no alcoholics, tobacco, coffee or tea; for these drugs aggravate the disease.
Two or three pints of water should be drunk each day.

Those who have had any experience with the average treatment can recognize the simplicity—and, if my statements are true.
the superiority—of my plan; indeed, the difference is as great as the
difference between barbarism and civilization

*The Present Plan of Treatment Anything but Aseptic.*—
The customary plan of taking care of the discharge is to advise the
Gentiles to wear a pledget of cotton over the glans penis, held in
position by the foreskin; and the Jew is sent away with a rubber
or muslin cot to hold the cotton in place; never a thought being
given to the infectious nature of the discharge, and the infection
that this treatment forces.    What would such treatment of wounds
lead to?    Would it be called aseptic treatment?    The customary
dressings prevent free drainage, and the more "cleanliness" on this
order practiced, the more surely complications will arise.    The
barbaric practice of wrapping or tying bandages on the penis to
secure cleanliness causes retention of the discharge and swelling of
the penis by interfering with the return circulation.    I have seen

dangerous infection caused by such interference with the circula-
ton; in one case gangrene, necessitating amputation of the penis.

All doctors know of the necessity for drainage in wounds,
and should know of the necessity for drainage in inflammations of
canals. Inflammations of mucous membranes, as well as wounds,
must be kept clean and the exudations removed as soon as they are
thrown out. I believe that all the complications that make gonorrhea "perilous" can be prevented by adopting these suggestions.

*Prolonging the Disease.*—There is a tendency for gonorrhea
to be prolonged in those who work hard or ride horseback. Those
who allow their minds to dwell on sex matters or indulge in intercourse, and persist in heavy eating or the use of alcoholics and
tobacco, need not look for a speedy recovery.

*Quick Relief and Cure.*—The disease will pass away quickly
and without a complication, if sufficient rest is had, the mind is kept
free from sensual thoughts, the eating is confined to a pint or a pint
and a half of clabber-milk three times a day, and a like amount of
water is taken during the day, and perfect cleanliness, according
to the above instructions, is practiced.

*Cause of Complications.*—When perfect cleanliness is secured
and the penis is allowed, by a rational dressing, to empty and clean
itself of all discharge, there will be small possibility of complications; but when the penis is abused by bandages or dressings that
prevent free and perfect drainage, and injections are given of drugs
which further irritate and denude the mucous membrane, look out
for swelling and ulceration of the foreskin; and when ulceration is
established, a continuance of the same treatment that forces this
state may cause ulceration and destruction of the glans penis, or
even the body of the penis.

I have had cases consult me with fistulous openings back of
the glans through which the urine found exit instead of passing out
through the mouth of the urethra, caused by ulceration forced by
obstructive dressings.    Plugging up the meatus with pledgets of
cotton held in place by the foreskin, or by rubber or cotton cots,
frequently causes ulceration and sloughing at the mouth of the urethra, after which there will be more or less obstructive, organized
stricture formed; or if a bandage is kept in place by a cord wrapped
around the penis, edematous swelling will take place, which of itself
becomes obstructive, forcing the discharge back into the deep urethra, infecting the urethra's full length, and causing inflammation
of the prostate and even the bladder.

# CHAPTER VII.

---

## PROSTATITIS.

---

*NFECTED PROSTATE* is very distressing, and should be treated by sending the patient to bed and fasting him for several days, or until he is comfortable and able to retain urine for three hours. To overcome the distress and frequent urination, the patient should have a hot bath of ten or fifteen minutes' duration three times a day. When relieved, his food should be toasted bread and butter, followed with a glass of milk. *Meat and potatoes should not be eaten until the disease is cured.* If there is retention of urine caused by swelling of the prostate, it will be necessary to introduce a self-retaining soft-rubber catheter, and irrigate the bladder every three hours at first, then three times a day, then once a day, as the symptoms demand. Don't use the catheter until the hot baths have failed to start the urine! To irrigate, use only warm distilled water; it is a mistake to medicate, as I have seen great evil follow the continued use of so *simple a remedy as borax.* As soon as the symptoms justify, the catheter should be removed. Great care should be exercised, in introducing the catheter, not to wound any part of the passage; for infection is liable to take place at every denuded point.

# CHAPTER VIII.

## Cystitis—Inflammation of the Bladder.

*ONORRHEAL CYSTITIS* is one of the greatest misfortunes; for there is a possibility of it never being cured. This complication may be brought on by carrying the infection with the instruments used for irrigating the bladder. The common practice of injecting the urethra is the cause of infecting the deep urethra, prostate and bladder.

*Treatment.*—The treatment should be rest in bed, no food for three or four days, except a glass of water, hot or cold, every hour or two. A hot bath of thirty to forty minutes' duration must be given once or twice a day until fully relieved; then the feeding may be a pint of clabber-milk three times a day, and positively no meat or potatoes so long as there is any sensitiveness in the bladder manifested by pain and frequent urination. As soon as the urethral inflammation is controlled, bladder irrigation may be given, not, however, unless there is retention of urine; for frequent, painful urination may be caused by prostatitis, not cystitis.

*When to Use Bladder Irrigation.*—If it can *positively be determined* that inflammation of the bladder exists, bladder irrigation should not be delayed; but irritation and inflammation of the prostate and neck of the bladder so frequently pass for bladder disease that the physician should be quite sure of bladder infection before he makes the mistake of treating it; for if it is not infected, it is liable to be forced to take on infection by the treatment. Real gonorrheal cystitis is rare and cannot occur except by the grossest malpractice.

In treating the bladder, use only warm, distilled water. Medicated douches are liable to set up inflammation of their own, which will refuse to get well. Rest in bed without food, or eat at most only a pint of clabber-milk three times a day, and hot-water irrigations. These suggestions make a dependable treatment when carried out carefully.

It should not be forgotten that when chronic diseases of any kind follow gonorrhea they are built by the treatment and not by the disease. This may appear so improbable to physicians who are used to looking for cures to follow drugging, and who believe that the tendency of the disease is to spread, that they cannot resist the temptation of modifying my treatment by adding drugs; but if they do, they need not expect ideal results, and, of course, they cannot hold my treatment responsible for evil results.

# CHAPTER IX.

## ORCHITIS.

HIS is the most painful complication forced on gonorrheal subjects. It is often brought on by astringent injections given for the purpose of drying up the discharge. Such treatment should be recognized as criminal and punishable; for it is liable to ruin the patient by bringing on septic rheumatism, suicidal mania as well as other manias, and heart disease (endocarditis) ; and sterility is a foregone conclusion.

### EPIDIDYMITIS.

Epididymitis is an inflammation of the seminal vesicles. It is not uncommon for orchitis and epididymitis to exist together, and so far as treatment is concerned, it does not matter which organ is inflamed. It is usual for sterility to follow inflammation of both of the seminal vesicles.

*Symptoms of Attack.*—This complication starts up suddenly. At first there is a heavy feeling, with sensitiveness on handling. The swelling often attains the size of a fist in twenty-four hours, and every increase in swelling adds intensity to the pain in the back as well as in the testicle.

*Treatment.*—As soon as this complication begins to set in, the patient should fast, drink hot water every hour or two, and take a hot tub-bath. The water should be as hot as the patient can endure, and he is to stay in the water until fully relieved, if it takes an hour or longer.   If the bathroom is close, leave the window and door wide-open, and have the patient sip cold water frequently to keep away fainty feelings.

Repeat the bath as often as necessary to keep the pain under control.   When better, food may be increased to toasted bread-and-butter, eaten dry, and followed by buttermilk or clabber-milk.

When the disease has been badly managed and suppuration takes place, of course the sooner the pus is let out through a good-sized opening, made with a sharp bistoury, the better; the opening must be thorough enough to secure a perfect drainage, otherwise the disease will drag and another opening will be necessary.

# CHAPTER X.

---

## STRICTURE.

---

I T IS said by those who are in a position to know that *80 per cent. of all cases of gonorrhea extend to the deep urethra at about the close of the second week or the beginning of the third.* I am prepared to prove that it is due to the treatment, and not to any tendency of the disease to go deeper.

Specialists declare that stricture is a well-known result of gonorrhea; I say it is not necessarily a result of gonorrhea; it more often results from the prevailing mode of treatment, and my contention can be proven by any physician who is willing to test out my plan.

Masturbation, and decidedly acid urine, such as heavy starch- and meat-eaters have, are both causes of stricture. Anything that irritates or denudes the urethral mucous membrane is a cause of stricture.

Stricture means a narrowing of the urethra from contraction of scar tissue. It does not occur except in those cases where the discharge has been held back and forced to take on decomposition —forced to change from a yellow, creamy, non-irritating discharge to a thin, greenish or brownish acrid fluid that is excoriating and highly septic. This discharge is destructive to mucous membrane, especially so when held on it by the usual dressings.

Experts declare that most strictures are located in the deep urethra. It is not my experience; indeed, I have been consulted by many who have been treated for stricture of this portion of the canal, and I have found one, two or three in the anterior and middle third, and none in the deep or posterior third.

Strictures are soft and easily managed when treated immediately after, or just before, the subsidence of the inflammation.

In treating strictures, or the granulations which are sequential to the inflammation, I use an olive-tipped sound about half the normal caliber of the urethra, and rub until the sensitiveness vanishes. This treatment should begin about the tenth day. The sound should not be pushed beyond the first third of the urethra until it is quite sure that the inflammation is gone.

In all cases of gonorrhea there are sensitive points left after the discharge has ceased. These points are folds, follicles and granulations—granular tissue—and their presence is known by symptoms of itching. There is an irresistible desire to rub the urethra, and patients should be permitted to rub to satisfaction; but they should be instructed to rub always toward the end of the penis, and not back toward the bladder. External rubbing or massage is necessary to overcome these sensitive points and to dislodge retained secretions in folds and follicles. The sound, properly used, is a better treatment and should be used daily; and as the urethra becomes less sensitive, a larger sound should be used until one the full size of the urethra is found.

### HOW TO USE THE SOUND.

*Sound Treatment of Strictures.*—Wash with hot water and soap a few olive-tipped sounds, as well as the hands; dry both on a clean, fresh towel, and dry-rub the sound with a fresh towel to make it smooth and bright. Have the patient urinate, and wash his penis with hot water and soap; then lubricate the sound with white vaseline, and introduce into the mouth of the urethra carefully, for it is very sensitive. Be sure to begin with a sound small enough. Rub back and forth, especially the sensitive points, and as soon as there is developed a toleration, use a size larger and still larger, until one is found that appears to meet with a slight resistance. This is my way for searching for strictures. Always begin with a small sound. The rubbing should be continued until all sensitiveness has vanished; then repeat the treatment every day, or every other day, until the urethra is normal.

When this treatment is first begun, it may produce a little discharge of bloody water or even blood. This should give no concern; for it means the opening-up of ulcerating folds and pockets, and the breaking-down of granulations, which is necessary to hasten a return to the normal state. At the first use of the sound, it should not be introduced more than two inches; then at every repetition of the treatment the sound can be introduced a little farther, until it is pushed to where the urethra curves under the pubic arch. Unless symptoms justify the invasion of the deep urethra, it is well to keep out of it. This part of the urethral canal is sacred—held so by nature, and should be by doctors. If, however, the unfortunate patient has been in the hands of a clumsy, so-called professional man, who has, by conventional treatment, driven infection into this part of the urethra, a curved, olive-tipped sound may be used in the same careful way recommended for the treatment of the first two-thirds of the urethra.

The sound rubbings should be continued daily until all sensitiveness is gone; and in all cases of organized strictures, resulting from maltreatment, the sound should be used until the stricture is sufficiently dilated and all soreness gone, after which a little of the same treatment can be given every six months or every year to insure a healthful state of the canal.    All that is necessary is to use the sound until the rubbings overcome irritation, chronic inflammation, or tumefaction and engorgement of the mucous membrane; for organized stricture, like all scar tissue, cannot be gotten rid of, and treatment should stop when all sensitiveness or active symptoms are gone; and if the stricture has not reduced the caliber of the urethra more than 25 per cent., the treatment need not be given except to correct sensitiveness.

## ORGANIC STRICTURE.

Organic stricture will give no trouble when there is no chronic inflammation of the mucous membrane; but when the caliber of the urethra is lessened from one-tenth to one-third by organized stricture, and one-third more from thickening of the mucous membrane —granular inflammation—there will be sharp pains experienced at times in urinating, caused by pressure on the sensitive granulations by the urine, which is more or less obstructed in its flow.   When there is much granular thickening of the mucous membrane, the urethra loses its power of self-cleansing; then the canal will become septic through putrefaction of the retained exudates, after which auto-infection takes place.   It is then said that gonorrhea has returned.   This chronic granular state may be forced to take on renewed activity by sexual excitement or a drinking debauch, or both.   The injury to these parts from sexual excitement and bruising adds to the already lessened caliber, and the more obstruction developed, the more retention of the exudation.   In this state the urine fails to keep the canal clean; for a sufficient volume cannot pass through the obstructed points to thoroughly wash out; hence putrefaction and fresh infection are liable to take place any time. A victim of this condition is capable of infecting or imparting gonorrhea, whereas only a short time before he was unable to do so, due, according to medical authority, to the alleged fact that the gonococci were latent or dormant. Indeed, they, as well as all kinds of germs, are always latent or dormant, or innocent, when their habitat is aseptic; but as soon as the secretions become putrescent, they become saturated with the septic poison, and then they are able to transmit infection. The tendency to return is not due to retained germs. Why are germs innocent today and infectious tomorrow? It takes abuse to bring on fresh engorgement and increa.ed secretion, then retention of secretions until putrefied, after which infection.

*Treatment.*—The treatment for stricture and chronic inflammation is to establish drainage as soon as possible by the following treatment: Have the patient bathe the penis in very hot water as often as possible; eat lightly, and when there is fresh infection take clabber or buttermilk three times a day, until the inflammation is controlled; wear a towel to catch the discharge. A sound should be used to disgorge the mucous membrane. Always have the patient urinate just before the sound is passed, so as to wash away as much of the accumulated discharge as possible. It may be well, for the first few days, to use a little cocaine for those who are very nervous and sensitive. Introduce a small amount of 4 per cent. solution with a glass tube; pass the tube down to, or below, the stricture, and inject it by having previously fitted to one end of the glass tube a bulb from a medicine-dropper. Hold the penis in such a manner as to prevent the solution from running out; then introduce the sound, and rub thoroughly. This may cause a sharp bleeding

in cases of long standing, where the mucous membrane is much
thickened, but no harm will come from it; indeed, the patient will
experience relief.   Possibly at the next urination there will be a
little smarting and burning, but the stream will be larger and more
effective in washing out and cleansing the canal.   Drainage will be
improved with every treatment, and a cure may be expected in a
reasonably short time.

## CHAPTER XI.

### Bubo.

ENLARGEMENT of the inguinal glands is a complication caused by maltreatment.

Inflammation of these glands never occurs in properly treated cases. It is infection pure and simple, and the infection is from septic absorption. Buboes can come from a suppurating inflammation of any part of the penis, if the cause be anything capable of starting up an ulceration, and the treatment be of a nature to cause the exudation to putrefy.

*Treatment.*—The physician should busy himself with getting rid of the point of infection. If there is swelling and ulceration of the prepuce to the extent of seriously impeding the return circulation, bathe the organ with hot water and soap; then follow with pure cold water, after which a very narrow, needle-pointed bistoury can be used to punch six to a dozen places in the preputial swelling; this should bring about relief of swelling. This small operation should be performed every day until the swelling is gone. As the swelling subsides, all symptoms will improve. The diet should be light; if the patient is full-blooded and heavy, he should fast until the symptoms are controlled.

Buboes often occur from ulceration of the foreskin brought on from neglect of cleanliness, and the malpractice of cauterizing practiced by doctors who have an idea that heroic treatment is necessary.

The treatment consists of bathing the penis with hot water often enough to keep the exudates from becoming septic. After washing, anoint with white vaseline or olive oil, and cover with gauze; then apply the towel to protect the clothing. Positively no bandaging or dessing that will impede the circulation.

When the bubo suppurates, the pus must be let out by a free incision—drainage when necessary—and dressed with vaseline, gauze and a suitable retaining bandage. The point of primary infection must be cured, or other glands will become involved.

# CHAPTER XII.

## CHRONIC CLAP OR GLEET.

GLEET ranges from a state where the discharge is almost nil to a full gonorrheal discharge. The latter condition should receive the same treatment given an acute gonorrhea; for in reality that is what it is, and it has been brought back by a reinfection, autogenerated.

The name "gleet" should be restricted to those cases presenting a slight discharge of a mucous or albuminous character. Where there is a yellow or brownish tinge, it indicates that there is enough inflammation to cause a necrosis of the mucous membrane, and that the point is dangerously near where reinfection will take place. All that is necessary is to neglect cleanliness and allow the meatus to close up, or retain the discharge by the use of the usual dressings.

Where the discharge is colorless, if the patient will stay from women and keep the mind free from the sex subject, all will be well in a short time. The sound should be used to rub and cause the granulations to be absorbed. Cleanliness must not be neglected even in health.

The cases throwing off a brownish, or greenish-yellow, discharge should be given as careful treatment as a fresh attack. These cases need careful treatment with the sound. Before the sound is used, the patient should wash with soap and water; then urinate. The sound should be introduced carefully, and all sensitive points rubbed until the sensitiveness is gone. The rubbing is a form of scouring; it squeezes pent-up secretions into the urethra so that they can drain and wash away. When well done once a day, it is one of the most potent, satisfactory and rapid curative agents that can be used. Of course, the patient must keep away from sexual excitement, eat lightly, abstain from all stimulants, and, neither last nor least, *keep clean.*

No greater care is needed in the treatment of an infected surgical wound than should be given to gonorrhea, and I am bold to state that the appalling results frequently experienced are due to the criminal ignorance or carelessness of the physician and his patient.

If the profession and the people can be taught to recognize gonorrhea as a septic infection, requiring as careful treatment as wound infection, we shall then be in a position to prevent the complications that are common to the present plan of treatment.

It requires maltreatment to develop chronic clap or gleet; or, as I stated at the first, if the disease is treated properly, there will be no complications. Those adopting my plan of treatment will not meet with chronic clap or gleet, except as patients come to them for treatment from other physicians.

## QUICK CURE.

Patients must be made to understand that if they wish to get well of an acute attack at the earliest possible moment, they must keep their minds free from thoughts on the sex subject; and if this is hard to do, a complete fast will make it easy. This is one of the most important items of information I shall give in the treatment, and it should never be forgotten.

In the chronic form of the disease patients must control their minds as well as their bodies. So long as a patient mixes with women, and permits himself to be sexually excited, he may as well indulge in intercourse. Indeed, abstaining from the act without controlling the mind is worse than indulging and keeping the mind free.

Men who are engaged to marry, and spend two or three evenings a week with their wives-to-be, will be hard to cure. The sex excitement will keep the sex organs in a high state of engorgement. Such cases often complain of "weak manhood;" of having a waste of semen. They have an albuminous discharge, caused by sexual excitement, which keeps them uneasy about themselves; it is due to mental, sexual debauching, and can be overcome very quickly by removing the cause; namely, keep the mind off of sex thoughts, and use as large an olive-tipped sound as can be passed every day. Each time that the sound is used the urethra must be rubbed, at all sensitive points, until all sensitiveness vanishes. The diet must be light: fruit for breakfast, vegetable soup for lunch, and toasted bread and a glass of milk for the evening meal. Stimulants of all kinds must be interdicted, for they keep the patient from getting well by keeping the sex organs in a state of hyperemia.

## RECURRENCE.

If those with chronic gonorrhea go on a debauch, they are liable to get up enough urethral irritation to start up inflammation any time: *then, if drainage is imperfect,* if the mouth of the urethra is allowed to glue up, and cleanliness is neglected, the discharge is liable to become quickly septic; after which auto-infection will take place, and the infection of others is possible, if intercourse is had. This is known as a return of the disease.

When marriage is consummated while the man is suffering from gleet, he should be very careful. If intercourse is indulged in, great care should be given by both, and especially by the husband, to be thoroughly clean, and if the mind is kept clear of the subject, he should get well quickly.

I do not recommend indulgence until, with the sound and proper living, the disease is positively cured. Intercourse should not take place except in full health; but if this rule is broken, it should not be oftener than once a week, and separate bedrooms should be occupied. If intercourse is to be indulged in, right or wrong, before indulging the penis should be washed with hot water and soap, and the urethra cleaned out by urinating. After the act, both should wash thoroughly, and the wife should use a douche after intercourse, and establish the habit of washing the genitals after every urination. Proper cleanliness is almost equivalent to immunization.

If cleanliness is practiced, there will probably be no infection. When the husband has a septic discharge (please remember that all discharges in chronic cases are not septic), he should not have intercourse; for the act engorges, inflames and forces reinfection on himself, besides unnecessarily exposing his wife.

If vaseline is freely used at all times, it is antidotal to reinfection; not, however, without practicing all other precautions.

# CHAPTER XIII.

—

## PREVENTION, OR ABORTIVE TREATMENT.

—

N ACUTE gonorrhea the mouth of the urethra should be kept well greased with vaseline to prevent it from becoming glued together. This stopping-up prevents the discharge from passing out, and the discharge, when retained, takes on a septic change in a very short time. This is especially true when the genitals are kept engorged from sexual excitement.

Those who make a business of exposing themselves should use vaseline freely, and for several days after exposure the mouth of the urethra should be well greased to prevent gluing up. Infection will not take place unless there is a slight abrasion, and if the abrasion is kept clean and well greased, the primary infection cannot spread by being reinforced by fresh auto-infection, but will soon subside. The disease is getting a good start when there is enough discharge to close the meatus. If urination does not occur oftener than once in three to five hours, and the meatus is closed by the gluing process for that length of time, auto-infection will take place very rapidly and a virulent disease develop. It takes from three to eight days to get up enough auto-infection to amount to a pronounced gonorrheal attack. If laymen knew just how infection takes place, they could prevent the development of a serious disease; but unfortunately people are ignorant of prevention, and believe that, when infected, there is no help except what the physician can do.

It is too late to ward off full development after there is enough irritation to attract the patient's attention to the penis; for then there is enough infection to cause a smarting, and, if examined, the mouth will be found glued together, and, by squeezing, one or more drops of pus will come out, which means enough infection to last several days, even if no more infection is permitted.   But as soon as this is discovered, a thorough hot-water-and-soap cleansing should be made, and a thorough greasing of the urethral mouth, to prevent gluing up.

### HOW TO PREVENT.

Suppose the patient could have known, after the intercourse, that he had been exposed to infection—his course would have been to urinate, wash and grease.   Then wash twice a day and grease, and use the vaseline after each urination.   The primary infection not being aided by reinfection, it would not amount to enough to justify so much trouble, if it were not that the trouble taken was the only reason that there was not much trouble.

The discharge that dries and adheres to the foreskin and glans penis is to be feared more than the fresh secretion, and that is why I advocate so much washing.

I would recommend that all men, who have had gonorrhea followed by stricture or gleet, make a practice of thoroughly washing the penis, urinate and use vaseline immediately before having intercourse; then follow with hot water and soap, and vaseline.

I do not believe that every intercourse with an infected subject is followed by infection.   Physicians seldom are infected, notwithstanding they are examining infected wounds and cavities of their patients' bodies daily. Of course, the hands are not so susceptible as the genital organs, and are washed infinitely oftener. However, an abrasion of any part of the body brought in contact with *septic* virus will be infected if the virus is kept in contact long enough to become absorbed; then, if there is an acid state of the secretions, the infection will work more rapidly in developing into a virulent type. Thanks to the natural resistance of the blood, only a small percentage of infections become systemic; if all should become systemic, the mortality from this cause would be appalling. No case of diphtheria, scarlet fever, typhoid fever advanced to a septic state, gonorrhea and syphilis, or wound infection, would recover.

### RESISTANCE GREAT IN A FEW.

Resistance is so great in a few subjects that all sorts of license can be indulged in for years before a first infection; after which, however, such subjects often find themselves victims of almost every exposure. When my attention was first drawn to this fact, I passed it as a coincident, but further observation convinced me that resistance can be great enough to almost amount to immunization.

People who habitually overeat, and are troubled with fermentation of food in the stomach, will develop such a vulnerable state of the body that they are easily infected, and infection is liable to become systemic. This is the class who die after injuries and operations, and when they contract gonorrhea or syphilis they must be very carefully handled or they will develop virulent types. They must fast and drink freely of water, until the disease is fully controlled; for this is the only way to secure the elimination necessary to control the disease—to control the disease in the shortest possible time.

### FOOD PREVENTS A RAPID CURE.

It should be generally known that an intake of food sufficient, under ordinary conditions, to nourish the body prevents rapid elimination, and if quick eliminative action is desired, a short fast, with the free drinking of water, is the surest way to bring it about.

# CHAPTER XIV.

## Not Self-Limited!

HE profession's loyalty to the germ theory causes it to believe and teach that gonorrhea is not self-limited; that the gonococci dot not disappear from the body as do other germs, but, on the contrary, *they burrow down in the tissues and may be inactive for months or years!* What of it? If they are inert—and they certainly must be, to lie dormant for months and years—what awakens them out of this hibernation? So far as I know, I have answered that question for the first time in the history of the disease, and a practice based upon my answer will forever do away with the infinite uncertainty, and the dread that always lurks in the wake of uncertainty.

Knowledge makes us free of the dread that must accompany all obscure subjects. If I am right, a definite cause and treatment are given to take the place of a cause that is not always a cause, and a treatment that is still in as much doubt and uncertainty as is the cause. When cause is positively known, the right treatment must be the natural sequence.

Those to whom I have confided my beliefs as to the cause and cure of venereal diseases have found fault with the plan, and declare it ought not to be true if it is; for, they say, those who have the disease should have it hard and long. I, however, do not believe that it is a physician's prerogative to add to the penalty that is attached to breaking health laws.

It is said by those who profess to know, that so long as there are shreds in the urine there may be blood-cells, and so long as there are blood-cells there are liable to be gonococci and danger from intercourse. I say: So long as there is a septic discharge there is danger of infection. I advise against intercourse as long as there is a septic discharge; for it should be the wish of everyone to get well as soon as possible, and not be the cause of infecting others. But if circumstances should make it *imperative* that a victim of the disease *prove his health* in from two to three weeks after careful and consistent treatment, he may proceed as follows, and have implicit confidence that he will not impart infection: Urinate, and follow this act with a thorough hot-water-and-soap washing of the genitals; then make free use of white vaseline.

A septic wound is made aseptic by washing off all putrescent material, and there will be no more septic material unless exudates are allowed to accumulate and be confined long enough to become septic.

It is general knowledge among the adepts in vice—especially those who are equally familiar with professional courtesans, and women of *respectability*, yet of easy virtue—that the chances for not becoming infected are ten to one in favor of the courtesan. The reason for this is that proprietors of bawdy-houses cannot afford to allow "gentlemen" to contract diseases in their houses; hence one of the cardinal *virtues* of these institutions is cleanliness. Besides, the woman who hopes to retain the privilege of an entree to the best houses must not be a means of infecting patrons. Hence, commercialism has really furnished the medical profession with strong evidence against its theory of venereal infection, but to no purpose, for none are so blind as those who will not see.

# CHAPTER XV.

## The Treatment of Gonorrhea in Women.

HE treatment of gonorrhea in women should be, first, last and all the time, cleanliness; a fast, or very little food; positively no meat—and this prohibition includes eggs; no alcoholics, tobacco, coffee or tea. The patient must wash the genitals at every urination, and change the napkin that often, if it is a little soiled. Three copious douches daily of hot water—as hot as can be borne—using a gallon or more of water each time. Should such cases have local treatment? Hands and instruments must be given a wide berth, if a quick and uncomplicated cure is hoped for; prodding around the vagina and womb with speculums, probes and dressing forceps is almost sure to drive the infection where it would not go if left *distressingly alone.* Meddlesome, clumsy and *officious doing something* is the cause of the alleged "Venereal Peril," as advertised by specialists who know no more of the cause of the "peril" than they do of a prevention and cure.

One eminent specialist in New York declares that "a man who infects his wife from a latent gonorrhea may receive a fresh, virulent infection from her in turn." But that doctor cannot explain why, and there is no explanation except that no amount of *septic* gonorrheal infection can produce immunization; for sepsis is the exact antipode of life, and there can be no compromise. It always possesses toxicity.     An infection today has no preventive influence for tomorrow, and that is why I do not believe in the so-called immunizing serum.    The time will never come when a human being can be made immune to infection, and, according to my view, there is but one infection.    An individual can infect himself and he can infect others, and he can come in contact with infection without being infected, unless there is an abrasion; and if the exudate that is thrown out from the abrasion is not allowed to dry and close the mouth of the urethra, or be bound on the abraded surface by dressings, long enough to force decomposition and absorption, auto-infection will not take place.

If gonorrheal infection is not followed by re-auto-infection, the primary infection will end quickly.    This leads me to the conclusion that a virulent case of gonorrhea is a case where there are daily and hourly re-auto-infections, and the proper treatment is such as would be successful in controlling a wound infection; namely, drainage and cleanliness.

# CHAPTER XVI.

---

## CHORDEE.

---

HERE inflammation is severe, and involves the minute ducts and mucous glands of the urethra, and spreads to the spongy tissue, a certain amount of agglutination takes place, which interferes with the influx of blood and with normal erections. Distention under these circumstances takes place irregularly, and causes a bending of the penis in the direction of that portion that does not distend fully. This irregular distention is accompanied with pain; for the part that does not become engorged is drawn like a cord to a bow, and when erections occur during sleep the patient will have such pain that it drives him up and out of bed before he realizes what is disturbing him.

Cold applications relieve quickly, but the trouble may return very soon after sleep comes again.

I have found the thorough use of the olive-tipped sound the most reliable palliative as well as curative treatment.

Introduce as large a sound (olive-tipped) as the meatus will take without causing great pain; pass it gently, rubbing every sensitive point until there is no sensitiveness left. This treatment establishes drainage by emptying the folds and ducts—pressing the accumulated discharge to the surface, where it can drain away or be washed away with the first urination.

Before the sound is used there should be an accumulation of urine in the bladder, so that immediately after finishing the use of the sound the patient can pass urine and wash out all the discharge that has been pressed into the urethra.

Where a patient is extremely sensitive or unwilling to bear a little discomfort, a four per cent. solution of cocaine may be used to deaden sensation for the minute the sound is being used. The cocaine should be carried in with a small glass tube, on the free end of which is fitted a rubber bulb such as is used on a medicine-dropper. The tube should be long enough to introduce to at least half the length of the urethra; to be exact, say about four inches long; then fill the tube half full and pass it gently in for about three inches, and as it is withdrawn the fluid may be pressed out by squeezing the bulb. As the tube is brought out of the meatus, the end of the penis is to be squeezed enough to prevent the solution escaping, as it will without this precaution. A sound should be ready to use at once; and it should be as large as will pass without force. As soon as the olive tip is in the mouth it prevents the escape of the solution. At once the rubbing may begin. Push the sound in and out, being careful not to allow the tip to come out of the mouth of the urethra, and at each movement pass it in a little farther, rubbing back and forth until the tip has reached the deep urethra, or about four or five inches from the mouth. Some judgment must be used. If the penis is pulled upon, of course this lengthens the canal, and the sound may go farther in before reaching the urethral curve.

If gonorrhea has been treated on my plan from the start, there will be very little, if any, chordee, and the sensitive portion of the urethra will not extend beyond two or three inches; but if the case has been treated in the usual way, the injections will have forced the infection, no telling how far, possibly to the full length of the urethra.

Where a patient has been treated on my rational and conservative plan, there will not be what is known as chordee; there may be a little discomfort from erections, but it will be due to granulations in the urethra, and will pass away after the first or second sound treatment.

The sound should be used daily until there is no longer any need, and cocaine should not be used where the patient can be induced to take the treatment without it; and when it is used, its use should be suspended as soon as possible, for it causes unnatural sensitiveness. If the treatment is given carefully, there will be no excuse for the use of the drug.

It should not be forgotten that the less the patient eats, the less pain he will have and the sooner he will get well. Those who eat heartily will be troubled with sexual desires, and this causes engorgement and delays the cure. Those who will not give up heavy eating, and will continue the use of tobacco and alcoholics, and mix with women, may keep the disease from getting well for weeks, months, and sometimes years.

How many physicians have watched a case of syphilis from its beginning to its end without giving a dose of drugs? Not one! Then what are their opinions worth? The first day a drug is given in any disease, that day the disease is masked—it ceases to be a natural disease—and no physician is wise enough to tell what symptoms are from drugs, what from food, and what symptoms belong to disease proper. As absurd as this statement makes the situation, the best physicians in the world demand that their opinions be taken on a subject that is masked, and as obscure as the incoherent mutterings of delirium.

In the first place, stop the expenditure of nerve energy; secure rest; feed the proper foods in proper quantities and in proper combinations, which gives necessary physiological rest; give the body proper care in bathing, rubbing and clothing, and then poise the mind. The whole of therapeutics is contained in that short outline.

*  *  *

The worst forms of syphilitic skin diseases are a compound of ignorance, bedrooms without ventilation, dirty beds, filthy underwear, no bathing, and harsh eating, mixed with physical degeneration from sexual debauchery.

*  *  *

Dirty beds, overindulgence in meat, bread, potatoes, coffee, tobacco and alcoholics, with neglect of body-bathing, can generate a disease that will equal the worst pictures of syphilis or bubonic plague. The cure, of course, means education and regeneration.

*  *  *

The treatment for any form of so-called syphilis is to secure rest for the nervous system; fast when in pain or discomfort; stop all stimulants; give the simplest foods—and have the foods properly combined: fruit for the first meal; bread and milk, or bread and vegetable soup, for the second; meat and salads for the third.

*  *  *

Where I look for the correcting of errors of life to cure my patients, physicians generally expect to correct all ill feelings by, in some mysterious way, neutralizing an obscure poison in the blood by drugs.

# Syphilis

## CHAPTER XVII.

### INTRODUCTION.

 YPHILIS is the king among blood diseases—so recognized by the medical profession. I recognize it as the climax of all *Mongrel Diseases*, from a physical standpoint; and from a psychical point of view it is the Don Quixote.

The profession saddles on syphilis everything that cannot be accounted for in a rational way. If a symptom presents that by exclusion cannot be attributed to any known disease, then it must come from syphilis, whether or not a scintilla of evidence can be discovered by all the Sherlock Holmeses of the profession. This accounts for all the insanity we see and hear tell of concerning the contagiousness of the disease—that the disease is caught from drinking-cups and kissing, and in many unsuspected ways. This insanity had to be built to save the syphilis fallacy. There was no other way to account for the unaccountable.

All diseases have a common origin, and syphilis is no exception to the rule. Location, the particular tissues involved, age, personal habits, and mode of living and treatment, all tend to modify and change the appearances of disease.

No disease has a single cause, but there is a general cause for all, on which minor influences have an individualizing effect.

## SYPHILIS A SKIN DISEASE.

Thirty years ago I had Fox's full picture gallery, and I looked upon those pictures as perfection from an artistic point of view, and as profound as truth from the medical-science standpoint.

I could not question the accuracy of the great professor's opinion of the diseases he illustrated so well in picture form. That those horrible diseases must come from some demon influence outside of the body was self-evident to my mind. It is strange how self-evident every impossible thing is to the uneducated, inexperienced and prejudiced mind. It is as greatly surprising to see and know how far a great profession can go in unfolding truths after truths to prove an assumed falsehood. The "FOOL'S Paradise" is built by first taking a falsehood, and then supporting it with all the truth and wisdom of the age.

Syphilis is a lie! The central thought that there is a mysterious entity—a germ—that causes syphilis is false; but around and about it has been built a world of wisdom. For years honest labor and the brightest intelligences have been struggling to prove the accuracy of the assumption that there is a disease, "syphilis." If man's education could be simplified, he would be saved the waste of a world of time and energy. At least nine-tenths of man's time is occupied in defending his inherited knowledge, which is based on what ignorance has declared were self-evident truths.

It should not be forgotten that self-evident truths are all right from the standpoint of their origin; but, like all knowledge, they must not be inflexible; they must be adjustable to new conditions, and, unless they are, they become lies, on which truth may lash itself into impotency in its endeavor to save.

The universal cause of all diseases is autotoxemia; and that one cause is the effect of three other causes, namely: enervation, faulty elimination, and auto-infection.

### THE CAUSES OF AUTOTOXEMIA.

Enervation is brought on from any influence that uses up nerve forces. When energy runs low, the elimination is imperfect, and this causes an accumulation of waste products in the body—or the subject becomes autotoxemic. When this state is developed, digestion and assimilation become imperfect; this means that the faulty elimination is added to by imperfect digestion, or auto-infection. In time a subject in this state will have enough self-generated poisons to account for every disease with which humanity is afflicted; and every one of these diseases can be ameliorated and cured, if taken in time, by simply going back to the beginning of the chain of causes and correcting all. In the first place, stop the expenditure of nerve energy; secure rest; feed the proper food in proper quantities and in proper combinations, which gives necessary physiological rest; give the body proper care in bathing, rubbing and clothing, and then poise the mind. The whole of therapeutics is contained in that short outline.

I realize how radical all this appears to the reader, but not to me; for I have been gradually coming to it for twenty-five years.

The poison of decomposition is at the bottom of all skin diseases. There are many skin diseases said to be syphilis; but, as I have stated above, all skin diseases have their origin in autotoxemia and from the poison generated in the gastro-intestinal canal—auto-infection. Every disease said to be syphilis originates in auto-infection, and their variation from ordinary diseases of the kind is due to the drugs used in treating them. Cleanliness, inside and out, should be the first prescription. These skin diseases yield quickly to fasting, and a warm bath every night. As soon as the disease is controlled, the patient may have toasted bread and butter, followed with a glass of milk, three times a day, to be continued until the skin is entirely well; then a diet of fruit for breakfast, vegetable soup and bread for luncheon, and meat, cooked vegetables and salad for dinner may be adopted as a daily routine.

The severest types of syphilitic skin diseases are a compound of ignorance, bedrooms without ventilation, dirty beds, filthy underwear, no bathing, and harsh eating, mixed with physical degeneration from sexual debauchery.

The more decomposition there is in the intestines, as an established habit, the more degenerate the type of skin diseases that will develop.

Dirty beds, overindulgence in meat, bread, potatoes, coffee, tobacco and alcoholics, with neglect of body-bathing, can generate a disease that will equal the worst pictures of syphilis or bubonic plague. The cure, of course, means education and regeneration.

The treatment for any type of so-called syphilis is to secure rest for the nervous system; fast when in pain or discomfort; stop all stimulants; give the simplest foods—and have the foods properly combined: fruit for the first meal; bread and milk, or bread and vegetable soup, for the second; meat and salads for the third.

It does make a great difference what foods are eaten together.

The mind must be put at rest, fear must be controlled, and every bad habit overcome.

# CHAPTER XVIII.

___

## Syphilis Defined.

___

YPHILIS is the king of specific diseases; it is supposed to be acquired by inoculation from a specific germ.

When any part of the body becomes the center for the development of septic infection, the type of infection will be in keeping with, and peculiar to, the location. A badly drained wound in the flesh will develop a true septicemia.

An infection from a septic material may be superficial and local—simply a skin infection—or it may be deep and systemic. When superficial and local, if the patient is in a normal state—blood normally alkaline and nerve resistance good—he may have a slight localized inflammation, that will pass away without more inconvenience than a little soreness and stiffness. But if the system is depressed—enervated—elimination bad, blood slightly acid, a local infection will take on an aggravated form. The tendency then is for the infection to take hold of the deep tissues; the lymphatic glands in the immediate neighborhood of the point of infection become infected, and from these local glands the infection may spread. From a local insignificant injury, strong men are sometimes forced to lose a year from business, and not a few lose their lives. The reader should see the similarity or resemblance between the action of septic infection, as described above, and what takes place in smallpox vaccination. When vaccination acts badly it is said the virus is impure. The truth is *the patient is impure.* Vaccine is *inert or it is septic.*

A little carelessness in the treatment of an infection, the first few days to a week, may mean lost health for a year or two, or death.

### SEPSIS IS OFTEN AUTOGENERATED.

Septic states may be, and often are, autogenerated—independent of inoculation from without. For example: Intestinal fermentation may start up from imprudence in eating—from eating a winter diet in hot weather; the irritation resulting may cause a rush of serum into the bowels, which washes away the decomposition by causing a diarrhea; the diarrhea may fail to flush out of the bowels all of the decomposition, and a part of it is retained and added to by more eating, which causes more decomposition, until the glands become infected; then the disease will be named typhoid fever. There are no set symptoms that can truthfully be named typhoid until septic infection is developed, and then there is no more excuse for an educated physician to allow intestinal auto-septic infection (typhoid fever) to generate in a patient, when he is called in time to prevent it, than there is for a knowing surgeon to allow septic poisoning to generate in a wound, or to allow a petty infection to spread and become formidable.

This reference to typhoid fever will be *poo-pooed* by those who believe that the disease must come from germs taken into the system; but I dispute this belief, and back it with forty years of arduous professional labor and observation—enough to entitle my opinions to have some weight where work, labor and painstaking observations are worth anything, and especially when these opinions are backed by a record of cures and preventions that would be convincing to the most sceptical. All I stand for on this subject has been verified by a record of twenty-five years, in which I have not allowed a typical case of typhoid to develop when called early; and, when called late, I have not failed to bring all symptoms depending upon septic absorption to an end within a reasonable time.

The strongest argument I can offer, and which I believe can be offered, in support of a theory of cause is, that a treatment based upon the theory, works. I shall not impose upon my readers by advancing ideas·that have not been tried out until the possibility of error is reduced to nil.

### ALL FEVERS ALLOWED TO RUN WILL DEVELOP SEPSIS.

All fevers that are allowed to run on indefinitely will take on sepsis. This should be avoided by controlling the disease! How? Remove the cause. *If there is no cause!* If there is a physician so simple-minded as to make the excuse that "there is no cause," he certainly should have a guardian appointed to keep him from doing the public an injury. "If there is no cause"—which is too absurd to even discuss—then one must be found and removed. If the cause is nerve leaks, stop them up; if the cause is an intake of food that is not suitable, and it is producing irritations that are met by sedative drugs, this is quite enough to hold the patient down until sepsis develops, and perhaps death.

Remove all causes; not *a* cause, nor *the* cause, but *everything* that holds the patient back and uses up nerve energy. And a wise physician should see dozens of causes to be removed, when called to see a very sick patient; for, *believe me,* something *never has, nor ever will,* come out of nothing.

Suppose, instead of irritation, ulceration and septic absorption in the intestines, as we have seen in typhoid fever, we have irritation, ulceration and generation of septic poisoning in the vagina, or underneath a tight prepuce. Is it impossible to generate sepsis in the vagina; under a swollen prepuce; in a urethra that has become so altered in its mucous membrane that its mechanism of self-cleansing is more or less destroyed? Is it a fact that secretions, excretions and exudations pent up, and drainage neglected, will end in the development of septic poison in one part of the body, and not in another, or develop some other sort of poison in another part of the body?

Animal fermentation—decomposition—is simply *decay*, and the product is septic poison. The locality in which the putrefaction takes place may give the process a local coloring, but the basic poison is the same, namely: *Sepsis!*

EFFECT VARIES WHEN THE OBJECT ACTED UPON VARIES.

Like causes produce like effects, and where the effects vary the object acted on varies. Putrefaction must be the same; while the derivatives may vary somewhat, their toxic influence must be the same, and what modification there is, must be forced by the varying character of the object on which the toxic influence is expended. For example: If a subject, full-blooded and plethoric, with an acid state of the alimentary canal, should have intercourse with a woman who has an ulcer of the uterus and an accumulation of secretions undergoing putrefaction, he is liable to be infected. With what? Septic infection, of course. If the inoculation is on the glans penis or on the foreskin, and it is neglected—if the penis is not thoroughly washed and anointed with vaseline and kept strictly aseptic—reinfection will take place often enough to break the body down, by setting up septic lymphangitis. This disease I am describing is called chancroid, and is not looked upon as a formidable disease. However, if one of these cases should afterward develop symptoms of locomotor ataxia, or any central nervous derangement, the physicians who treated him for chancroid will be compelled to say that it was a case of mixed infection; that true syphilis was masked by the other symptoms. There is no proof of this; but it has been assumed that locomotor ataxia is almost positive proof that the subject has had syphilis, and that any previous sore on the penis, a gonorrhea or an abrasion, must have been accompanied by syphilis—the disease being declared a mixed infection.

If the exposed individual had been normal, instead of plethoric and autotoxemic, he probably would not have developed a sore of any kind on his genitals; or what sore there was would have been insignificant. (See Chancroid or Soft Chancre, page 100.)

### PROFESSIONAL SUBTERFUGE.

Mixed infection is a professional subterfuge. It makes a very weak point in a generally weak theory. The loophole, mixed infection, is as plausible a refuge for a disconcerted contestant as is the astute invention, *Typhoid Carriers.* I do not believe the profession is conscious of its irregular and guerrilla style of defending its so-called science. It is forced by its confusions to make explanations that do not explain, *except to those who are not troubled with thinking.*

The very fact that one, or one thousand, of the best physicians on earth *can't determine positively that a given case is really syphilis* ought to be proof sufficient that there is something desperately wrong with the *Syphilis Theory.*

Common sense must declare that a specific disease is specific because of its invariable action under like conditions; but this is not true of the disease called syphilis; indeed, it is anything but true.

Perhaps my readers would like to ask what I believe, or if I deny that syphilis has an existence. I deny that there is a disease "syphilis" other than a septic poisoning which develops from filth and nerve degeneration brought on from satyriasis.

### HOW THE HARD CHANCRE IS DEVELOPED.

Let us consider another class of victims. This time the individual is of average health and cleanly personal habits; bathes frequently, and is given to frequent promiscuous cohabiting; at times repeating the act often enough to cause chafing, which results, in the course of time, in the developing of a hardening or an induration on any part of the penis, usually on the glans. The induration may be quite small; in reality it is similar in nature to a corn on the toe, and, like the corn, it has been produced by chafing; no doubt an acid vaginal secretion has an indurating effect. One among the women visited by the subject has an indurated neck of the womb— a *hardened neck*—and, being passionate, she holds the subject in such a violent embrace that the penis is more or less injured, and chafing and indurating result.

Writers attempt to show that a hard chancre requires twenty-five days to develop. This is purely arbitrary and fictitious; for the class of men who *contract syphilis* would have to be sent to jail and a guard set to keep them away from women twenty-five days. To charge a suspicious intercourse, indulged in twenty-five days before a chancre develops, with being the cause of its development, is as far-fetched as to single out one of twenty-five drinks, in a drinking bout, as being *the one* that caused the drunkenness.

I have not been consulted by a supposed syphilitic who was not a libertine, and, instead of going twenty-five days without intercourse, such men come nearer having intercourse fifty times in the length of time their supposed chancres are. developing. Under such circumstances, is there anything strange about a chancre, or corn, being developed on the penis at some point where the greatest pressure or friction is brought to bear, both in intercourse and in chafing against the clothing? If the friction is great enough to abrade the surface, and the intercourse is with a woman who has chronic clap, or a uterine or vaginal ulceration, a local infection will take place, and, unless strict cleanliness is maintained from the first, a severe chancroid may develop, and if the victim is sufficiently enervated to begin to show central nerve lesions, then the doctor may decide that he has a mixed infection. If, however, no rawness or ulcer manifests on the chancre, and no constitutional derangements develop, the chancre will be passed as of no significance; but if symptoms produced by debauchery coincidently develop soon after the chancre, then of course the case will be defined as a well-marked syphilis, and what licentiousness has not already done toward breaking the victim down, *fright* and the *usual medication* for syphilis will finish.

### THE DON QUIXOTE OF DISEASES.

Syphilis is truly the Don Quixote of all diseases. It truly represents a professional monomania. The profession has given so much study to the subject that it has become a real insanity. Why? Because of the fixedness of the cause. The premise is that the cause is specific, and it is a mind-upsetting task to undertake to fit a fixed cause to a set of symptoms that are paradoxical as well as heterogeneous. How could such a long study of a subject, with a

fallacy as the central belief, end in anything else than insanity?
The fatal part of the whole study of so-called syphilis is that it
starts with the assumption that the disease is specific.   Here is
where the mistake is made, and nothing can ever come of the world
of study given the subject so long as the premise remains what it is.

If the disease has a specific origin——if it is caused by a specific
germ——why are nearly all important questions regarding the disease
still in dispute among high authorities?

If it is a disease presenting three stages, why do not those three
stages develop?

The syphilis of today is not the syphilis of the days of King
David; for the type of disease he describes is more that of soft
chancre or chancroid.   The refining has been going on so long that
what is known as real syphilis today has nothing in common with
the syphilis of old.   The old syphilis was a modified septic infection, and occasionally cases develop that equal the worst of the old
types. Bubonic plague is a type of the old syphilis. There is history
of a type of the disease that killed large numbers of people during
the reign of Charles VIII.

# CHAPTER XIX.

## GLANDULAR INVOLVEMENT.

IT IS said that within two weeks after the hard chancre has developed, the neighboring lymphatic glands become slightly enlarged and very hard. These glands are painless and never suppurate. Who is willing to say the glands were not enlarged before there was a chancre? I am not. I find people almost daily, who have enlarged inguinal glands, who never had a chancre or any venereal disease. Adenitis is not uncommon, and to find enlarged glands in the groin is not significant of syphilis; for they may enlarge from a sore toe, or they may come from decomposition in the intestines.

In about a month after the glands enlarge, an eruption appears scattered over the body. There are several kinds of eruptions, declared to be distinctive, but they are usually caused by the drugs given to these patients, or by the autotoxemia they suffer; besides, such patients are frequently troubled with so-called uric-acid eruption, and when drugs are given, the characteristics of this food-poisoning eruption are changed, and will appear in all the forms described as specific, or belonging to syphilis.

There are described rheumatoid pains and headache. Who has not seen the same in heavy eaters with sluggish portal circulation?

Falling of hair certainly does not belong to those who have or have not had syphilis. Many diseases cause the hair to fall, and a strict scalp disease, caused often by neglect, is the common cause.

So far as iritis is concerned, it can come as a result of enervation from excessive venery and autotoxemia. I know from experience that a syphilitic history is not necessary as an excuse for developing the eye diseases.

## MUCOUS PATCHES.

Mucous patches are said to be one of the characteristics of the disease. This is not true, for they are frequently found in the mouths of people who have no venereal disease—people who eat too much starchy foods and keep their stomachs in an acid state; just the class of people who take mercury badly, and in whom mercury starts up a lot of ulcerations of the mucous surface of the body.

The mental depression that many suffer, when told of their misfortune, will cause so much change in nutrition that the health frequently runs down for a year or more from this cause. What is lost in this way is often made up for by the continence practiced. Feeling that their lives have been ruined by their sexual debauching, a few become continent, and in a year or two rebuild a better state of health than they had for years before their ruin by syphilis. These are the people who are said to get well before having to go through with the tertiary symptoms.

Physicians expect a lull in the disease at the end of a year; and I know from observation that the lull, so-called, will prove a cure, unless the patient falls back into his old habits of debauching; which if he does, he will develop all sorts of diseases that the Don Quixote, Syphilis, will assume belongs to his realm.

Every part of the body contributes its mite to the great Quixote. If there is an uncommon symptom, it matters not what kind, it belongs to him; and, of course, all blood and glandular symptoms are his. Not any derangement of bones, joints, tendons —in short, not anything developing in any part of the body from whatever cause—but will be declared SYPHILIS, and treated as such.

Every one of these symptoms can be built without a chancre. How do I know? Because I have been treating the disease, for the past twenty-five years, just as though it had no existence, with the result that, when patients follow instructions, they get well and stay well, and fail to develop all the so-called stages.

### IS THERE ANY EXCUSE FOR SYPHILIS?

I am treating now not fewer than a half-dozen cases of loco-motor ataxia said to be produced by syphilis. An excuse for the disease—a cause great enough to account for the disease—need not be looked for beyond the daily lives of the subjects. Every one has abused himself sexually; indeed, the history of such cases usually reads about as follows: "I began at eight years of age to masturbate, and kept it up once to half a dozen times a day until I began visiting women, and have had intercourse once to four times every twenty-four hours for the past twenty years." Does such an individual require syphilis to paralyze him? Add to this abuse wrong eating, tobacco and often alcoholics, coffee and tea, and can any sane man believe that syphilis is necessary to add to all that crime against health, to make a successful ataxia?

Please bear in mind that there are many men who would out-rage their health as greatly by indulging sexually once every other day as others would if they should indulge twice each twenty-four hours. Sex power varies greatly. It is a power that should be conserved.

Can any sane man believe that the drugs usually given for syphilis are the proper treatment for a person cursed with all the habits to which I refer?

A profession is certainly obsessed when all these important items in a patient's life are ignored, and cause is declared to come out of the obscure, mysterious and extraneous.

### WHAT ARE PHYSICIANS' OPINIONS WORTH?

How many physicians have watched a case of syphilis from its beginning to its end without giving a dose of drugs? Not one! Then what are their opinions worth? The first day a drug is given in any disease, that day the disease is masked—it ceases to be a natural disease—and no physician is wise enough to tell what symptoms are from drugs, what from food, and what symptoms belong to disease proper. As absurd as this statement makes the situation, the best physicians in the world demand that their opinions be taken on a subject that is masked, and as obscure as the incoherent mutterings of delirium.

I have not given a dose of drugs in the treatment of so-called syphilis for fifteen years, and the consequence is that the great Don Quixote, Syphilis, has disappeared from my mind. Once he was a very great reality; today he is a memory. Since giving up the use of drugs entirely, pronounced syphilitic symptoms disappeared and took their places among symptoms that naturally follow errors of life. Those masked with drug action soon cleared up and pointed to their origin.

All symptoms not masked by drugs point to their origin and their cure; hence, physicians stand in their own light when they persist, day after day, in obscuring the symptoms of disease by developing drug diseases.

Since giving up drugs I have learned that all formidable symptoms known as constitutional syphilis are compounds of fear, wrong life and drugs, and are very easy to overcome when I can have the patient's help—when the patient is willing to give up bad habits and learn to live normally and naturally.

Gummy tumors, when they really have an existence, can be overcome by correcting the patient's nutrition.

Because of the profession's habit of obscuring all diseases by drugs, it cannot have any idea what influence sexual excess, tobacco, alcoholics and overeating of stimulating foods have on the organism. Where I look for the correcting of errors of life to cure my patients, physicians generally expect to correct all ill feelings by, in some mysterious way, neutralizing an obscure poison in the blood by drugs.

I know there are no obscure poisons in the blood; for, if there were, I could not cure my patients, for I do nothing in the line of attempting to overcome a syphilitic infection.

I could prolong this essay, and take up every so-called obscure symptom, and show the fallacy of conventional beliefs; but what is the use? Those who will see this subject with me do not require me to do so, and those who will believe me stupid and unscientific will not be convinced "though one rose from the dead!"

# CHAPTER XX.

---

## SYPHILIS AS I HAVE FOUND IT.

WHAT is syphilis, as I have found it?

It is a weaving together of a belief in a mysterious poison that contaminates the life-blood to the extent that all future life will be more or less handicapped by ill-health; that the bringing forth of children must be given up, or take the risk of leaving them branded with a father's vice and cursed all their lives; that, although well as far as appearances go, yet there is a possibility of infecting loved ones by a kiss or by the use of eating utensils. These beliefs cause nervous, imaginative persons to build a living hell for themselves. To this hell of fear, which is desperately enervating and ruinous to the digestion and elimination, there is added the cursed drug habit, that cannot do less than further ruin nutrition. This is the psychology of syphilis; after this state is built, perhaps there are people thoughtless enough to recognize it as a desperate and incurable disease! It will certainly prove to be, so long as the numerous causes and the misnamed cures, that build the disease, are used to continue its farcical treatment.

Victims of this psychical state get to be monomaniacs; they think of nothing else; they talk of nothing else; their opinions are reinforced by every doctor they meet. As fast as fear develops degeneration, it is pointed out as another proof of the ravages of

syphilis and the truthfulness of the *early diagnosis*. A real diagnostician would rather have every one of his victims die, those
whom he has declared would, than to have them live, if by living
they refute his prognosis. Pride in diagnosis has consigned millions
to a living hell; for the doctor would rather be right than to have
any patient get well who, he has said, could not get well.

I have seen splendid men ruined for life because *they knew*
their lives were ruined; not fewer than twenty-five to fifty first-class
physicians had told them so in the preceding fifteen to twenty-five
years.

What does such a state of mind bring on its victims? Arterio-
sclerosis, locomotor ataxia, and other forms of diseases peculiar to
premature aging. Nothing ages so rapidly as fear, unless it is
anger.

# CHAPTER XXI.

## Syphilis of the Nervous System.

HAT can be done for such people? Is there a cure? Indeed there is, if taken before monomania has become an organized change—before there are nervous changes that are permanent. A belief in constitutional syphilis, when once established, is a mania that cannot be cured.

The literature that has grown up around so-called syphilis, or syphilitic nervous diseases, would make miles of pages; but, on account of the central error, all must be wrong. The diseases described as due to syphilis can, every one, be accounted for when such causes as fear, drugs, errors in eating, overstimulation by coffee, tea, alcoholics and tobacco, and sexual abuse, are considered.

The disease known as chancroid—which is truly syphilis, if we are justified in giving the name "syphilis" to any so-called venereal disease—should be treated exactly the same as a local septic infection; for that is what it is.

The so-called real chancre comes from causes already mentioned, and develops in a more intelligent class—a class of men who are, as a rule, scrupulously cleanly; and that is why they develop the so-called hard chancre, while less cleanly men develop the more formidable-appearing local disease.

The soft chancre belongs to younger men—men who have not gone the pace; whose sexual excesses have not yet begun to develop symptoms of nerve degeneration. It is true a few break down early, proving that "It is not the distance but the pace that kills."

The hard chancre is aristocratic; it has class to it; it means the victim of it has lived a life filled with luxury, and has a mind satiated with sexuality in all its esthetic belongings, up to nerve degeneration. These diseases—nerve degenerations—should be treated from the standpoint of excess, and not for syphilis.

### TREATMENT FOR LOCOMOTOR ATAXIA.

When locomotor ataxia is beginning to send out its first symptoms, I use an olive-tipped sound to rub out any sensitiveness of the mucous membrane of the urethra, and to overcome strictures if there are any. I have found that an irritable urethra is often one of the exciting causes of ataxia. The mechanical irritation caused by excessive venery creates a sensitive urethral mucous membrane, which an acid urine aggravates, and causes much reflex irritation of the spine.

For diet, see Treatment of Syphilis.

All nerve leaks are to be corrected, and especially the large one, *Fear*. All stimulants are to be proscribed, and if their proscription throws the patient into misery, he should be sent to bed, with enough artificial heat to keep him warm, and he should be given to understand that the price of health is to suffer as much as necessary while nature is readjusting. It must not be forgotten that the belief in syphilitic inoculation is often the last straw to be added to a pronounced enervation, from years of excess, to bring complete nervous prostration. Sexual excess is the leading cause, but overeating, improper eating and the use of stimulants—alcohol, tobacco,

coffee and tea—add their influence.    After a man is once broken
down, if the fear of syphilis be added, the load is almost more than
an ordinary constitution can endure, and to recuperate requires time
and relief from fear.

### TWO FORMS OF IMPOTENCY.

Where impotency takes hold of these subjects early, they are
saved the *coup de grace*—syphilitic infection.    Perhaps I would
better say that when impotency is marked by inability to have an
erection, these subjects are saved the development of a chancre or
*corn;* while, on the other hand, impotency is frequently marked by
priapism; this is where the victim is cursed by constant erections,
and he fancies he is a satyr in strength, and he creates enough friction, if he can find women to indulge his impotent cravings, to work
up a *Hunterian chancre* that will satisfy the most exacting experts
on the subject.

I have been consulted by libertines who have acknowledged to
continuous friction in intercourse, of hours' duration.    On my ex-
pressing surprise that a woman could be found who would stand for
such treatment, I was told: "She loves me, and is so anxious to
satisfy me that she would not protest if I should be with her all
night."    Such fiends have boasted that, if it were not for becoming
raw or excoriated, they could continue the sex act indefinitely.
This statement was made to prove that they were very powerful
sexually, but proves, to anyone who knows, that they were badly
enervated and in reality sexually impotent.

Is there anything so very far-fetched when I accuse these
people who have chancres of having corns?

Is it strange, when these enervated people are told that they have syphilis and are given enervating drugs, and not one of their bad habits proscribed, that they develop all sorts of derangements?

The proof that I have to offer that there is not anything to the syphilis insanity is that I have no trouble in curing all such cases in a very reasonable time, where my directions are followed; and there are no relapses or after-effects.

# CHAPTER XXII.

## Treatment of Syphilis.

I F THERE is a chancre, keep it clean and anointed with vaseline.

Assure the patient, if it can be done honestly, that he can get well if he wants to, and almost as quickly as he wants to. If he is too heavy, put him on an exclusive fruit diet for a week or more; it will be well for him to remain on fruit until his weight is brought to normal. He should have a five- or ten-minutes' hot bath before retiring, followed with a cold sponge-bath, and another bath of the same kind in the morning after exercising vigorously for ten or fifteen minutes.

If there is a tendency to constipation, a pint of warm water should be drunk before breakfast, and a half-pint of water a half-hour before the noon and night meals.

When a case is suffering from pain of any kind, nothing should be taken into the stomach except water until comfortable, even if it requires several days to get rid of the discomfort.

When comfortable, eat fruit until the weight is normal; then eating should be restricted to fruit for breakfast; vegetable soup for luncheon; and meat (any kind except cured meats), cooked non-starchy vegetables* and a salad for dinner.†    A salad should be eaten daily with every dinner.

Tobacco, alcoholics, tea and coffee must be given up.    As much open-air exercise as possible should be taken.    The sexual nature must be controlled.    The mind must not be allowed to dwell on sex subjects.

This, no doubt, will appear to physicians as doing almost nothing for *a disease that requires skill to treat to a successful termination.*    To all who hold such opinions, allow me to say that there is no curing agent outside of the natural recuperating power of the body.    Allow me to go farther: There is no mysterious entity—germ—that has entered the body that must be killed, coaxed or driven out by drugs.    If there is infection, it is of a septic character, modified by the secretions peculiar to the genital organs, and should be treated locally as an infection, and not as a mysterious, specific disease, foreign to the environment in which it develops.

---

*See page 104.
†See page 107.

# CHAPTER XXIII.

## MERCURY IN SYPHILIS.

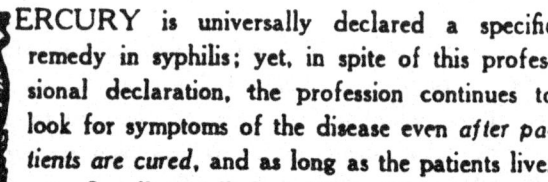ERCURY is universally declared a specific remedy in syphilis; yet, in spite of this professional declaration, the profession continues to look for symptoms of the disease even *after patients are cured*, and as long as the patients live.

In all so-called syphilitics there is, in the first place, pronounced enervation, and, as I have pointed out, most of the malignant cases have sexual impotency, which indicates a profound enervation. With enervation developed to such a marked degree, it is self-evident that elimination is badly interfered with, and gastro-intestinal digestion much impaired. As a result of digestive impairment there is a constant auto-infection going on from absorption of decomposition in the intestines.

No drug known to the profession is so powerfully antiseptic as mercury, and that is why it has been settled upon as *the specific* for the treatment of this disease. The profession built better than it knew, however; for it gave the drug for its supposed action on the mysterious, occult, syphilitic poison, and because of the drug's influence over the auto-infection, causing an amelioration of the symptoms, the profession naturally decided that the drug really controlled the syphilis. The mistake is natural enough for a profession to make that has itself persuaded into believing that disease is an entity that enters the body from without, and that self-generated diseases are impossible.

Mercury does not always act kindly, and the reason for its irregular action is that, when a patient is badly starch-poisoned, the drug will produce salivation; that is, the mouth becomes sore, the lymphatic glands enlarge, and, if the drug is continued over a long period, the whole body will suffer more or less from the poisonous effects of the drug. But I am forced to declare that these symptoms of poison are strictly those caused by mercury. When there is really septic infection, the mercury fails to salivate. Where the mercury has the greatest toxic effect is where there is the ordinary acid fermentation. However, the drug does control, for the time being, septic, as well as other, fermentations, and to that extent gives a short palliation. If those who give mercury really understood what it accomplishes, and then would make its administration no longer necessary by correcting the bodily derangements—the enervating habits—by teaching the importance of an orderly life—by teaching the correct care of the body, both hygienically and dietetically—they would have no trouble in curing every case of syphilis calling upon them.

# CHAPTER XXIV.

## To Correct Auto-Infection.

STOP all food except fruit for a few days. If the bowels are constipated, drink freely of water while on the fruit diet, and, if necessary, wash out the bowels with two-quart enemas of warm water. Pears are more laxative than other fruits. The small, seeded fruits, like berries, are constipating; while the bowels are sluggish, these fruits, and raw vegetable salads, and all the dairy products, except butter, should not be used, because they are constipating.

If there is a bad odor to the gas, or discharges from the bowels, fruit, and no other food, should be given until the bowels are thoroughly cleaned out and the bad odors entirely gone; then fruit should be continued for breakfast; vegetable soup,* bread* and butter for lunch; and for dinner, meat—lamb, chicken, fish, eggs or nuts (pecan); with the meat, cooked non-starchy* vegetables and a salad.*

Those who are over weight should take a cold sponge-bath* every morning, and a five minutes' hot bath, followed with a cold sponge-bath, every night before retiring. They should wear light-weight underwear the year around. In cold weather, enough wraps to keep warm.

---

* See pages 103 and 104.

# Formulary

Those who are thin, nervous and cold should not use fresh fruit; they should eat sweet, cured fruits for breakfast, such as figs, dates and raisins—not more than two ounces of either at a breakfast—and follow with a glass of clabber-milk, buttermilk or tea-kettle tea.* Precede the cold sponge-bath with a short hot sponge-bath.

Keep the feet warm. If necessary, have a jug of hot water in the foot of the bed every night.

These patients must have sleep. Those who cannot sleep—those troubled with insomnia—should be sent to bed for a week or two—long enough to bring on relaxation and sleep; then they should retire early. They should avoid excitement and becoming too fatigued.

_____

*See page 107.

# CHAPTER XXV.

—

## Chancroid or Soft Chancre.

—

HANCROID is the most common venereal disease. It can be brought on by anything that will cause an abrasion of either the glans penis or the foreskin.

Where the foreskin is long and rather close, there is a tendency for an accumulation of secretions to take place under it, and these secretions in time will ferment and start up irritation; inflammation follows, and then ulceration; and this is what is known as soft chancre. If it is maltreated, the base and edges can become indurated or hardened, and the glands infected; for pus or sepsis will develop in a sore of this kind, unless kept aseptic by frequent bathings.

An abrasion from any cause neglected and allowed to ulcerate, then badly treated with astringents *and even caustics*, as doctors frequently do, will develop quite a formidable-appearing disease. What is the difference between this disease and the hard chancre?

Those with the soft chancre are young men of full habit of body; they are young and have plenty of resistance; and if they were as cleanly as they should be, they would not develop such a disease.

Those with hard chancres are a class of men who have been *going the pace that kills*, until their nerve energy is used up and they have lost all resistance, and are just about to develop diseases that come from degeneration of the nerve centers.  But enough!  (See pages 79 and 80.)

To repeat:

Chancroid is an ulcer of the genitals caused by lack of cleanliness.

To prevent, the genitals should receive as much care, in washing and bathing, as the face and hands.  Those with a long prepuce are liable to have decomposition of the secretions that accumulate under the foreskin.  This decomposition often lights up inflammation.  The parts, unless treated right, become excoriated from the acidity of these retained discharges.  Unless cleanliness is begun at once, ulceration will take place, and the simple inflammation may, in time, be transformed into a septic inflammation, after which the inguinal glands will become involved and often ulcerate.  A few of these cases become systemic, breaking down the general health—the glands and blood becoming involved.  There is no need of this disease becoming systemic, and it cannot unless badly managed.

*Treatment.*—Cleanliness.  Hot water and soap should be used often, when the disease has a good start.  After washing thoroughly, a little white vaseline should be used.  Where the glands have become involved, the general health should receive attention; a light diet and rest, until the disease is controlled, and then, if cleanliness is practiced, there will be no return.

# Formulary

---

SPECIAL INSTRUCTIONS.

*Cold Bath.*—In the summer take ten minutes' exercise before bathing; in the winter take the exercise after the bath. If reaction is not good, use hot water first, and then the cold water; then, if the extremities do not warm up, stop the cold water.

### COLD BATH.

Take the bath as follows: Draw four or five inches of cold water into the bath-tub, and begin by washing your face and hands while you are still standing on the outside of the tub. Carry the water up over one arm and rub with your open hand; repeat until the arm is used to the cold. Then treat the other arm the same way. Then step into the tub, and treat each leg the same way. Then squat in the water and give your *genitalia* a thorough bath. Then drop on your knees and carry the water over your body; step out of the tub, and follow with a thorough dry rubbing with a towel. At night, before you go to bed, give yourself a five minutes' dry-towel rubbing, if you do not take a five- or ten-minutes' hot bath. Sleep in a nightgown or pajamas, and in a thoroughly ventilated bedroom. When the cold bath is followed by cold feet and hands, it should be preceded by a hot bath of three to five minutes' duration. Draw a little hot water and wash face, neck and hands; then step into tub, and allow the feet to toast for a few minutes; then follow with the cold sponge bath as directed above.

### HOW TO MAKE TILDEN TOAST BREAD.

To a quart of white flour, or equal parts of white and whole-wheat flour, add salt sufficient, a heaping teaspoonful of baking powder, two tablespoonfuls of melted butter; make into a dough with milk (unskimmed). Bake in the form of a loaf or biscuit. When baked, wrap in a cloth and put away until cool; then slice and return to oven, and toast; or you can have this bread made in the form of biscuits. When they come from the oven they should not be more than an inch thick, baked to a good crisp crust, bottom and top. These biscuits can be split and toasted for future eating.

\* \* \*

### HOW TO MAKE TILDEN VEGETABLE SOUP.

*Positively no meat or meat stock.*

Take equal parts of four or five of the following vegetables: potatoes, turnips, carrots, cabbage, spinach, onions, green peas, beans, or corn; run these vegetables through a vegetable mill; put to cook with enough water to prevent burning, and, when tender, reduce to the consistency of soup by adding boiling water. Season with salt and butter. Those in full health can use hot milk to reduce in place of water.

\* \* \*

### A LIST OF THE NON-STARCHY VEGETABLES.

Turnips, carrots, cauliflower, beets, cabbage, onions, summer squash, parsnips, spinach, tomatoes, lettuce, cucumbers, green peas, string beans, celery, asparagus, corn on the cob, kale, salsify, endive, egg plant, dandelion, and all kinds of greens.

My use of the word "non-starchy" is purely arbitrary, for the fact is there is starch in all vegetables.

### DECIDEDLY STARCHY FOODS.

I class as decidedly starchy foods everything made from grains—wheat, rye, corn, barley, rice, tapioca; also the Irish and sweet potatoes, dry beans and peas.

\* \* \*

### DR. TILDEN'S FOUR ESSENTIAL RULES.

The following four rules are as necessary as anything I shall ever be able to tell a patient; and, if patients desire to live long and well, they will certainly have to learn to live without breaking them:

RULE No. 1. *Never eat when you feel bad.*

You may not understand what I mean by "feeling bad." When you get up of a morning and you are conscious of not having rested well, and you feel heavy, tired, dull, cranky, nervous—go through with your prescribed morning routine, but DO NOT EAT BREAKFAST. Take a glass of water every hour or two during the forenoon. Then, if you pass through the entire forenoon feeling all right, you can have your lunch. You must feel well from one mealtime to the other, or miss your meal, even if it makes you weak to go without food. The more of this discomfort you have, the more evidence you have that you need to fast.

When you cannot miss a meal without feeling uncomfortable, you have chronic irritation of the stomach, and the more you go without food the sooner you will be well.

\* \* \*

RULE No. 2. *Never eat when you do not have a keen relish for food.*

When mealtime comes, if it is a matter of indifference whether you eat or not, do not eat.

RULE No. 3.    *Always avoid overeating.*

\* \* \*

RULE No. 4.    *Thoroughly masticate and insalivate your food.*

If you will masticate your food thoroughly, you are not very liable to overeat.

\* \* \*

### HINTS FOR THE SICK AND WELL WORTH REMEMBERING.

Always eat your bread and butter BY ITSELF, MASTICATING and insalivating each morsel until it is liquefied in the mouth.

### FOR CONSTIPATION.

Between getting-up time in the morning and breakfast time, drink a pint of water, cold preferred; and another pint before each of your other meals.    This will tend to keep the bowels regular. When going without food, take a glass of water every hour or two.

If the bowels are somewhat constipated, remember that spinach and onions are more laxative than other vegetables.

### WHEN NOT TO DRINK WATER.

Do not drink cold water for three and one-half to four hours after your meals.    If you must drink during this time, take a glass of *hot* water.    Cold water checks digestion.

### THE FOODS THAT ARE CONSTIPATING.

Keep in mind the fact that all the dairy products except butter, and all raw vegetables, are constipating; hence, when there is a sluggish condition of the bowels, stop the use of these foods until your bowels are regular.    Eat freely of the cooked non-starchy vegetables.    See list.

r as follows:
Fruit and the dairy products.
Bread, cake or dry cereals; butter, milk and ice-cream in hot weather.
Meat, cooked non-starchy vegetables and salads.
I have learned from experience that these are the best combinations.

\* \* \*

### TEAKETTLE TEA.

One-third milk, two-thirds boiling water, and enough sugar to please the taste.

\* \* \*

### TILDEN SALAD.

Take equal parts of fresh, crisp lettuce, tomatoes, and cucumbers or celery—enough to fill a dinner plate when chopped coarse; add onion to please, and dress with salt, olive oil, and lemon juice.

# Syphilis

BY

## R. L. ALSAKER, M. D.

EDITED BY

## J. H. TILDEN, M. D.

# CHAPTER I.

---

## SYPHILIS.

---

THE regular profession is as insistent on discovering *Specifics* as the geographical societies of the world have been insistent on discovering the earth's poles. The reward is so great, in money and fame, that there are many competitors and of necessity a great variety of characters and many directions are taken. Remedies are discovered in two ways; namely, how to aid nature, and how not to handicap her. For, be it known to all minds able to receive it, nature cures or there is no curing done. All that a cure can mean is the evolving into a normal physiological state, after, from whatever cause, the physiological balance has been lost. And disease is caused by any influence that perverts the normal, and if the normal is kept in a state of perversion for any great length of time, the functional changes that have taken place require time, after the cause is removed, to evolve back to the normal.

In spite of the truth that every process in nature is going forward or backward in an orderly manner, we have a large per cent. of people, even doctors, who believe in chaotic creation, such as the possibility of "making a three-year-old colt in a minute." In other words, they believe in snap-shot cures where nature requires much time.

The profession is now in a frenzy over the discovery of a specific for syphilis; its chemical name is Dioxydiamidoarseno-benzol; for short it is called Arsenobenzol, and shorter still, please know it by the name of "606;" later still: "Salvarsan."

It was discovered by Paul Ehrlich of Germany, a scientist of world-wide fame. How a man can become famous and be so illogical in his conclusions regarding cures is one of the grotesque psychological features of this day and age.

It is said that Dr. Ehrlich announces to the world that he has discovered a specific for syphilis that will cure "while you wait." Just drop off the car and have a little "606" injected into your gluteus and then hop back on the car and hang on the strap if you should find it uncomfortable to sit down while the drug is curing you.

When rational beings can be so educated out of common sense as to expect to cure disease in such an absurd manner, there is no hope that a rational system of cure will be evolved very soon.

Such diseases as syphilis and scrofula are known as blood diseases, whatever that means; the real disease is a perversion of nutrition, hence, imperfect blood making with a subacute lymphangitis, all brought on by septic absorption. This disease does not differ from other diseases produced by septic absorption except as the glandular secretion in the location of the initial lesion stamps its individuality on it. Of course, the resistance to septic absorption is greater in some localities than in others, and this will account for the malignancy of infections at times——the severity of the disease depends upon the amount of septic material absorbed.

If the physicians had nothing to contend with except a specific taint in the blood——a specific germ, if you please——then if it were possible to inject a germicide that would *really* kill the germ, a snap shot cure—"a cure while you wait"—could be made; but such cures are delusions—inexcusable delusions.

It is time the medical profession was getting wise to the fallacy of killing germs in the blood, and it should know that to correct a septic infection requires time; the body must have time to evolve enough resistence to nutralize the poison.

It appears that scientific members of the profession must cure on the spot or not at all. Why can't those who assume to teach be possessed of a little common sense? Disease evolves slowly; cures must be in the line of evolution.

The evolution theory is the nearest approach to a reliable synthetic philosophy known, and if applied to the present theories on health and disease will help the professions to bring harmony out of existing chaos.

If it is possible to square a system of cause and effect and a corresponding cure to universal philosophy, it would be proof of the correctness of the plan, and until the profession of medicine leaves chaotic reasoning and takes up philosophical reasoning, the present haphazard and guesswork will continue to reign.

Whenever one of the profession's scientists discovers a specific. it creates as great an excitement among doctors as the discovery of the sheath and hobble skirts created among women. Just now the majority of the medical profession is hysterical over the alleged discovery of another specific—another sure cure for syphilis. Mercury has been its sheet-anchor for years and the only acknowledged specific for the disease. Isn't it strange that almost the entire profession should be thrown into a frenzy over the discovery of a new cure when it was already in possession of a specific—a sure cure? And so sure is it of its ability to cure diseases that it is asking for federal power that it may force its theories on the public.

"606" is the name by which this new specific is introduced, because it is said to be the six hundred and sixth experiment of its discoverer. If this scientist will accept a friendly tip, which, if observed, will benefit him, I will say that he can extend his experiments to 6006, and he will find no specific; for he is on the wrong trail.

The principal drug in this *mystical prescription*, if the name has any significance, is arsenic. It is rather surprising to be told that a pathology peculiarly fitted to the supposed therapeutic action of mercury can be corrected by arsenic, but when we remember that it is the "regular" school of therapeutics that has discovered this new *sure cure* we should not be surprised at anything unreasonable if not impossible in the line of therapeutics.

This new remedy gives the doctors another *specific*. It would be well if this new remedy would prove to be more specific than the preceding ones, but in spite of the assurance that *we can depend upon it to cure syphilis*, we have specialists—doctors who make the treatment of this disease a specialty—telling us through books and periodicals that of all diseases this is the Nemesis; that its health-destroying influence is appalling. They tell us that society is honeycombed with its victims; that we are on the brink of physical damnation because of its ravages. This too in spite of specifics!

This dread disease should be wiped off from the face of the earth! There is certainly no excuse for its devastating ravages when all of the leading physicians of the "regular" school declare that mercury is specific, and now another specific has been discovered that cures *quickly;* in fact, "while you wait."

"606" is creating almost as much furor as did Brown-Sequard's "Elixir of Life." This elixir was made from the reproductive secretions of some of the lower animals and was one of the scientific delusions of the age. Many readers should remember the Pentecostal-like awakening and conversion this *specific* had upon the members of the medical profession. From the most humble to the highest in the profession not a dissenting voice was raised, but with universal accord, and as one voice, all declared "Eureka." It certainly was a specific according to the "regular" medical standard for the promulgator of this elixir died a short time after making his discovery, and this is positive proof, according to this science, of the specificity of a remedy. This elixir was declared to restore youth to the aged and virility to the impotent. Within a few weeks after the eminent French physician announced his new discovery there was no question but that the "Elixir of Life" had been discovered, for the rank and file of the profession had proven it. It should not be forgotten that the press and public opinion, then as now, were in accord, and gave the *nonsense* dignity by their endorsement.

It is well not to forget that it was the same profession, press and public opinion, that are now demonstrating such zeal in honor of the new discovery, and they are just as sure that this discovery is specific as they have been that every other discovery was specific; we are assured that "606" will do just what is claimed for it. All that is necessary now is to have the Government patronage for which the A. M. A. is praying, and it will do away with syphilis, and put disease and death out of business! Then syphilis will be a thing of the past! Just how it is going to do all this grand work is hard to tell, if we judge the future by the past. But possibly it has succeeded to an adeptship we know not of, and can now use "606," vaccine, antitoxin, mercury, quinine, and other *invariable specifics* to prevent and cure disease.

Unfortunately the specificity of this last cure will be like all of the *cures* offered by allopathy, namely, a specific failure. How do I know? Because syphilis is not a specific disease, hence, it can not be cured by a specific remedy. It is a disease that good health will prevent and cure. Those who are most susceptible to the diseases known as gonorrhoea and syphilis are starch poisoned and mercury makes a splendid ally.

This new cure is being tried on innumerable cases of chronic syphilis, and, if we believe what we hear, *it is producing wonderful results!* Isn't it strange that there are so many cases of chronic syphilis to experiment on with this new cure when they have all been cured by the use of mercury?

This remedy, like thousands of others that have been *discovered* by the "regular" profession, will pass, and that, too, at no far distant day.

Syphilis is as easily cured as any of the common diseases met with day after day, if it is taken *before it is cured by mercury.* There is a mercuro-syphilization brought on by the administration of mercury for its cure that can not be cured; those who would avoid this dread disease should sidestep doctors who are so infantile in their thinking as to believe in the specificity of drugs.

J. H. T.

# CHAPTER II.

## Ignorance of Syphilis.

HIS is a disease that should be better known to laymen than it is, but a false sense of modesty—prudery—has kept the knowledge from the public. If young men and women knew more about the true nature of the so-called venereal diseases there would be fewer of them. If parents did their full duty they would instruct their children regarding their sex natures so that when they reach puberty the dangers menacing those ignorant of the sexual life would be entirely overcome. This would be far superior to the present haphazard system where the children, especially in the large cities, receive their education in this line from the most ignorant of their playmates and often from perverts or degenerates who are older.

What is more beautiful than the manifestations of life? Watch a plant as it modestly peeps through the ground in the spring; it first puts forth one or two little leaves, then grows a sturdy stem, then blossoms and finally develops its fruit. Is there anything vulgar or obscene about it? Is there anything about generation, the explanation of which needs to bring a blush of shame to any cheek?

The development of a human being is much more complex and wonderful than plant growth, and fully as beautiful and sacred. Why a large part of the public should object to an intelligent discussion of any part of human development is difficult to comprehend.

Disease of one part of the body is as disreputable as disease of any other part. All diseases are due to the mistakes we make. Men in high stations of life and ladies of gentleness and refinement do not hesitate to discuss their digestions, headaches and rheumatism and expect sympathy. But let one of them say that he is suffering from syphilis and see how quickly he will be ostracized, notwithstanding he may not have sinned more than the others. To the physician in general practice there are no aristocratic maladies, nor will there be to the laity when they gain a proper understanding of what disease is.

Laymen do not have enough knowledge of this particular disease to exert their usual salutary influence upon the profession. It is a fact that the people compel the profession to step up and take more advanced ground each decade which results in better treatment. The tendency of all large organized bodies of men is towards inertia. It is so much easier to practice in the old way. Medical men, as well as other people who cater to the public, must furnish what the public demands or lose their patronage. As soon as the public grows too intelligent to submit to a given treatment the profession is compelled to give it up for something more pleasing. It is a matter of evolution and can be observed in the toning down of church creeds and the changes in legal procedure which secure more justice and less obnoxious law. It was popular clamor that forced the profession to cease venesection, to quit salivating patients with mercury, and to discontinue giving harsh emetics and the big doses of nauseous drugs. If the filthy serum treatment is ever given up it will be after the public has demanded its relegation to oblivion.

Doctors do not as a rule give out any information on venereal diseases. Lately the newspapers and magazines have had a great deal to say on the subject because of Ehrlich's discovery of "606." Usually the public gets its knowledge from glaring advertisements in the newspapers, with headlines as follows: "Men! I guarantee the cure of all blood diseases!" Above this announcement appears the picture of a benevolent looking bewhiskered man who calls himself a doctor. This vampire gets hold of the young men who have been unfortunate in contracting, or thinking they have contracted, syphilis or gonorrhea (the so-called blood or venereal diseases) and he keeps on *curing* them until they have neither money nor health left. This is the method of the advertising quacks. The ethical quacks have a much smoother graft, as we shall see later.

For centuries syphilis has been a puzzle. We are not even sure what the word is derived from. It is said to be derived from two Greek words meaning hog lover.

Some claim that it is a comparatively modern disease, while others say that it is as old as history; the latter view is probably correct. About the time America was discovered an epidemic swept over Europe and for this reason America has obtained the unenviable reputation in some quarters of giving syphilis to the old world. The people in the south of Europe blamed the French and called it the French disease. In other countries the name of some other nation was given to it. In one thing all nations agreed, namely, that they themselves were not to blame, that it was due to foreigners.

During the middle ages people were extremely filthy and their morals were in keeping, for immorality and filth are synonymous. Hence it is not surprising that syphilis flourished. There were, history says, nineteen to twenty thousand leper houses scattered over Europe for the accommodation of those who were afflicted with leprosy, but on account of the loose methods of description it is hard to tell whether they harbored lepers or syphilitics.

Mercury was used in this disease four hundred years ago and today is considered one of the specifics. No matter how skeptical the medical man is of drugs, he generally believes in mercury for syphilis, quinine for malaria, and antitoxin for diphtheria.

. We are told that until a few years ago no one knew the immediate cause of syphilis. But now we are told that it is caused by spirocheta pallida, a specific germ which gains entrance through abrasions and wounds, especially on mucous surfaces! This germ causes all the symptoms grouped together under the name of syphilis, at least so we are told.

This would be a very satisfactory solution of the trouble if it were true, but it is not. It is as impossible to have a typical case of syphilis without the routine medication these patients are put through as it is to have a typical case of typhoid fever without scientific nursing, medicating and feeding. One can see what a deleterious effect mercury has on the tissues by noting how soon large doses salivate those who take it. History tells of people who lost their teeth and even parts of their lower jaws through taking this drug.

The claim now is that mercury kills the spirocheta pallida, but it must be given from two to three years to do its work; and then it must be given again whenever the patient shows any signs of any kind of disease, in spite of the fact that it is said to have once cured the disease. When an individual has once had syphilis all his subsequent ills can be traced to this cause, in spite of being cured with mercury. Medical logic is accommodating.

If mercury is powerful enough to cause necrosis of the jaw bones, it certainly is corrosive enough to cause degeneration of other tissues, especially when given for years. To the ruinous action of mercury is added that of the iodine salts. The iodides (generally potassium iodide and sodium iodide) are very irritating and soon upset the stomach. But the word has gone forth that the iodides remove the pathological deposits caused by syphilis, so they are given in spite of the fact that they derange digestion.

Within the last few months another specific has taken the center of the stage. Where it has taken mercury two or three years to "cure," this one, arsenobenzol or "606," is said to do it in a few days and with only one injection. It is claimed for this latest remedy that it will cure those cases where mercury has failed. How could mercury fail if it is a specific?

This goes to show how little real meaning can be attached to scientific medical phraseology. A specific is a remedy that cures a certain disease. What are we going to do with the cases where the second specific fails, and failures are already recorded? And what does cure mean? A patient is cured of syphilis and in five or twenty years he returns and is to be cured all over again. If one is unable to make good on his medical pretensions, he should be possessed of linguistic dexterity.

We are said to have only three remedies—*sure specifics*—and they fail not only sometimes, but often. For a while Professor Ehrlich's praises will be sung, and then the people and the profession will wake up to the fact that they have been "stung."

Why do we have so many apparent cures following the injection of "606"? Because after its use the doctors leave their victims alone and that is often all that is necessary for a cure. Usually there is not enough arsenic in a dose of "606" to do any material damage, and the benefit is due to the fact that only one or two injections are used.

The readers will please bear in mind that the most striking and most widely heralded discoveries made in the field of therapeutics during the last few years have been of remedies which are given only once or twice. Before antitoxin was introduced the little ones who had diphtheria were treated and nursed to death. As soon as antitoxin gained professional confidence the sufferers were given the number of units the medical man considered necessary, and this was seldom repeated more than once. What was the result? When the children were let alone they were given an opportunity to recover; antitoxin got the credit for being curative, when in fact the only service it performed was to encourage the doctors and nurses in keeping their hands off. It is on the order of the Christian Science cures, which take place because they do not antagonize nature in her efforts at throwing off disease.

Many physicians firmly believe that mercury and the iodides are the proper remedies. It will probably take a long time for this fallacy to die out, for it has gained respectability and credence by several hundred years of use. So firm is the belief in the efficacy of iodine for the removal of pathological developments that it is even applied over tubercular glands with the idea that a cure will ensue. Trade customs, whether in selling short weight groceries, short measure dry goods or bogus cures, die hard. The more ridiculous a belief appears to be the more adherents and defenders it apparently gains.

Syphilis is a filth disease. Those who keep clean and have clean habits are in no danger of contracting it. By keeping clean I do not mean merely to keep those parts of the body which are exposed to the air free from filth; it is most necessary to keep the bowels and blood clean. This necessitates right eating, drinking, breathing, etc. Those who are constipated and consequently suffer from autointoxication react much more severely to any form of infection than those who keep their bodies wholesome. There are many "whited sepulchers" walking about, and these are the people who have serious attacks of whatever diseases they unfortunately contract.

Syphilis is primarily a local irritation. In typical cases nature makes a decided protest against the entrance of the infectious material into the system, as manifested by a hardening of the initial lesion, which is nothing more than an induration or hardening of the tissues at the point of irritation, a sort of breastwork made up of white corpuscles which have been exuded or thrown out to prevent absorption and keep the disease local. When the ulceration is not kept clean, the decomposed exudates are absorbed, infection takes place and travels along the lymphatic vessels to the lymphatic glands, which are those in the groin, because of their close proximity to the primary sore. If it is satisfying to anyone to call the specific infection spirocheta pallida, all right, but I will firmly take my stand on this proposition: The germ, if there really is a causative germ, need not be brought to the part by contact with the disease. If the local conditions are favorable for its development it will develop without any external aid. The glands of the groin will enlarge and if enough mercury be given a real case of syphilis with all its complications will develop.

The fact is that syphilitic infection acts the same as any other slow infection and there is no need of iodides,, mercurial or arsenical compounds, like "606" (latest name salvarsan), for its cure. Keep the local abrasion clean, so there will not be a decomposition of the exudates, and there cannot be an infection.

If a case is treated right and mercurials not used the horrible group of symptoms we associate with a typical case will not develop. There will be no skin eruptions,. no mucous patches, no prolonged night pains, no falling of the hair, and no gummatous formations with the destruction of bones and cartilages. Allow me to repeat, it takes a good doctor and orthodox treatment to develop a clinical picture of typical syphilis.

The mercurial diseases established by using this drug are legion, and much harder to cure than if the so-called chancre were left to lay ignorance; in fact the greater danger in the disease called syphilis is mercury, but it is as hard to eradicate the mercury superstition from medical minds as it is to get some people to disbelieve the doctrine of infant damnation.

If infection takes place the nearest lymphatic glands begin to swell and if improper treatment is continued there will be no reason why the whole lymphatic system shall not become involved contaminating the entire blood supply and paralyzing nutrition. It truly becomes a toxemia. But this is true of other diseases where there is constant irritation with absorption of the decomposed exudates.

If one has an initial abrasion or injury the proper thing to do is to keep the sore cleansed and free from irritants. No mercurial salves or washes are necessary. Then clean out the bowels and keep them clean. If there is a tendency towards constipation, regulate the eating so that this will be overcome. It is absolutely necessary to correct dietetic errors, and to give food suited to the individual. Most people who contract syphilis have been careless in other ways, and they generally dissipate in either eating or drinking, or both. This should be stopped. In short, syphilis should be treated the same as any other disease; the cause must be removed and the patient should learn to take care of himself. Mercury never did help anyone, but it certainly does build future trouble, trouble which is harder to correct than the disease for which it was given.

Not long ago a case was treated at our offices; it came from one of Denver's specialists who had pronounced it syphilis. The young man said that the doctor had "found some of them corkscrew germs" (spirocheta pallida, so-called cause of syphilis). He was told that it would require two and one-half to three years to cure him. He was given mercury tablets and these he began to take before he applied to us. The drug caused him to suffer pains and aches all over. I prescribed a fast for twenty-four hours and directed him to clean out his bowels. Within forty-eight hours he was free from pain. When he followed instructions he got along nicely, but when he broke over he had a return of the disagreeable feelings. People who really wish nature to cure them of this trouble, or any other, must give nature a chance.

One of the very sad features about syphilis as we know it is that the unborn generations are liable to suffer from the malpractice to which the parents have been subjected. People treated along natural lines will not have tainted babies after they once have allowed the poison to work out of their systems, and if for no other reason it is surely worth while to treat the body in such a way as to restore it to the normal again, which can not be done with drugs. Mercury prevents the elimination of the toxic materials and causes a degeneration of cell life, resulting in such a lack of vitality that babies born of such parents are either sickly or die before or soon after birth.

Considering the disgrace, sorrow and suffering syphilis has caused, surely it merits the earnest attention of sensible people. But if we are to be misled by every new specific that is foisted upon us, the problem will be no nearer a solution in the year 2000 than it was in 1800.

# CHAPTER III.

---

## ETIOLOGY.

---

AUSATION is a subject of the greatest importance. Upon a correct interpretation of cause depends the successful treatment of all diseases. In guiding the sick back to health, a great deal of faith in, as well as a knowledge of, nature is necessary to give one who is a member of the small minority the courage to contend for the right. Numbers help to make belief respectable and no matter how fallacious an opinion is, if it is backed up by a numerous following, its advocates feel a sense of security that comes from knowing that many believe as they do.

This is true in all walks of life; even doctors like to be on the popular side. The majority wields such a social influence that it gathers the richest professional rewards. The few who dare to differ materially from their fellows succeed in making themselves odious and become targets for malice and misrepresentation; after they are dead, their work will often be appreciated, often appropriated without credit, by those who furnished the jibes and jeers for the forgotten. If they fail to reap their just reward, there is a little consolation in the fact that they have prepared the soil well and planted good seeds for others to harvest.

There is nothing else that will give a physician so much confidence in himself and his treatment as a thorough belief in the correctness of his etiology.   If the causes of disease are not correctly understood, the treatment will not be suited to the case and cures cannot be expected.

In no other department of medicine is the profession so much at sea as in etiology.   If one is willing to take a critical view of the subject, it will be seen that the ideas of causation have not advanced in two thousand years.   True, they had no miscroscopes then and were therefore unable to talk of bacilli, spirilla and cocci; but they believed disease to be an entity which, in some mysterious way, entered the body and took possession thereof. That is exactly what is meant by bacteriology and is believed today by the vast majority of the "regular" profession.

What difference does it make whether we believe that one is possessed of devils, evil spirits, miasma or of diplococcus intracellularis meningitides?   The basic fact remains that in either case we have the fallacious idea that disease is due to extraneous agencies over which we have no control unless we are smoked, pickled or canned.

The discoverer and founder of Christian Science believed in malicious animal magnetism which is the same as demonology and hagiology, but clothed in different words.   The theory of bacterial causation of disease is merely a belief in malicious vegetal and animal influences, for the so-called pathogenic microorganisms are of vegetable and animal origin.

It is very comforting to people to think that no matter what befalls them, they are not to blame.   It is also a consolation to the profession to know that a microorganism so small that it would take perhaps ten thousand laid end to end to make one inch can come floating through the air or be taken in with one's food and drink, and settle in one's anatomy and cause disease.

All the germ has to do is to start dividing and redividing and soon there will be a family that would embarrass even a Roosevelt. The so-called disease-causing (pathogenic) germs reproduce themselves by the simple process of splitting, and in a very short time there are millions where there was only one, providing the surroundings are favorable. If the germs were the real cause of disease, that is, if they were capable in themselves of producing disease, this earth would be populated by them. Certainly there would be no people.

Physicians who believe that microorganisms cause disease naturally are on the lookout for remedies to destroy the germs. The result has been that all sorts of chemical and animal antiseptics have been discovered! We now have antitoxins and serums for the treatment of diphtheria, typhoid fever, meningitis and other diseases, and neither last nor least, a complex chemical compound for killing the spirocheta pallida. The profession takes this last bait as innocently as though it had not been angled on the same hook hundreds of times before.

The germ theory of disease is very plausible, it is simple, and what is most important of all, it is a mind saver, for it saves one from thinking. The bacillus typhosus causes typhoid fever, they say, and that is the end of it. This is a much easier solution than analyzing the patient's mode of living and finding wherein he does wrong; how he has broken down his resistance and become susceptible to disease influence. If a theory is to be accepted by the multitude, it must be either so complex and involved that no one can understand it, or it must be so simple that they do not need to think about it. Whether it is right or wrong makes no material difference in the results of the treatment.

No one who has looked into the subject can deny the existence of different forms of bacteria. They are part and parcel of life and exist everywhere; in fact, they are necessary to the higher forms of life. They are a part of nature's economy. They are utilized in the process of higher evolution, and again, they help to bring highly organized bodies back to their original elements. The fact that they are present and necessary should prove that they do not cause disease any more than did the omnipresent devils and demons of ancient days prove that they were the cause of disease. Popular opinion was just as sure of its beliefs then as it is today, and was more arrogant and dogmatic.

The fact is that microorganisms cannot cause any particular disease except where there is obstruction to physiological functioning. When normal functioning is impaired from long overwork, or the nervous system is exhausted by worry, fear, anxiety, sorrow, grief, or over-excitement; or from injury by accident or design; enough poison has been generated to reduce the life forces and make the body a victim of its own environment, then the system is in a favorable condition for bacterial activity, but the bacteria are a result, not the cause of these conditions.

If there is one ailment of which doctors speak with certainty, it is tuberculosis. It is said most assuredly to be caused by the tubercular bacillus. But is it? No, it takes a great deal of abuse to the body to so weaken it that the tubercular bacillus can do it any harm. No one has or ever will see a sufferer from tuberculosis who did not have his nutrition ruined by digestive disturbances and the digestive derangements precede the tuberculosis months and often years. Often neither doctors nor patients are aware of this. Frequently patients have gorged from the time they can remember, and have never really known what it was to feel well. The doctors have been too busy building theoretical cures and compiling statistics to match, prescribing tuberculin, feeding milk, eggs and other good, nourishing foods, to take time to give the victims of the disease the personal attention necessary to get at the root of the malady.

To declare that a tubercular bacillus starts housekeeping in the lungs and then tuberculosis develops requires a great deal of imagination and a very large lack of observation.

The cause of syphilis has eluded the laboratory physicians until recently it has been decided that a specific germ has been discovered, the spirocheta pallida, which is said to be the cause. There is no doubt that there are germs present in syphilis the same as in all other diseases, and we must not forget that they are present in health. The germ has been found in the lesions time and again. But its presence does not prove anything except that it is present. Do not forget Typhoid Mary and other carriers. Soon it will be proven that there are but two classes of people so far as the doctor is concerned, namely, one class that carries germs and is well, and another that carries germs and is sick. Soon one class will be in the hospital and the other in quarantine.

The diphtheritic bacillus, or one that cannot be distinguished from it, can be discovered in the throats of people who are not sick and also in the throats of pneumonia patients, and yet there will be no clinical signs of diphtheria. The pneumococci can be so plentiful that it would be difficult to make a thorough culture test from the mouth and throat without starting a pneumococcus colony; yet, we do not all have pneumonia. If everyone who eats and drinks of typhoid bacilli were to contract enteric

fever, our blessed profession would be so busy treating these
patients that there would be no time left to lobby with politicians
to secure legislation against quacks.

The *post hoc propter hoc* argument used to establish bacterial etiology in other so-called germ diseases is also used in
syphilis. It is not more reasonable here than in other diseases,
nor does it square more with facts. We have an opportunity to
judge of the correctness of a proposed treatment when given the
etiological theory on which it is based. We have a right to question the merits of a treatment when we know that all previous treat-
ments based on the theory have been failures. Mercury is said
to kill the spirocheta pallida, yet it has to be given for years.
Why should it require from two and a half to three years to
kill the spirocheta pallida with a drug that is said to be a specific
or antidotal to this germ? If there is any truth in the theory of
toleration, the germ should be able to establish a toleration for
mercury in that time. On the other hand, a treatment based on
the idea that syphilis is caused by bad habits will eradicate the
disease entirely in a reasonable time, without any relapses.

What is the cause of syphilis? There is not one cause, but
many. It is brought on by the same causative factors that bring
on almost any disease, such, for instance, as pneumonia, eczema
and catarrh; of course, there must be a localizing, exciting cause,
a local irritation.

The primary sore is caused by a local abrasion; then irritation, uncleanliness and an acid state of the secretions does the
rest. Located as it generally is on the genitalia, imperfect drainage results in infection of the lymphatics in the groins. In reality,
these glands act as inhibitors of the infection. They stay the
progress of the toxic absorption and in so doing they become in-

flamed and swollen. This will be explained more fully in treating of the pathology of the disease.

After infection has taken place, the patient, if under regular medical treatment, is medicated with mercury. This drug produces degeneration which only adds fuel to fire, for the whole syphilitic process is one of degeneration. It must be remembered that syphilis under the treatment of regular physicians is given the regulation or orthodox treatment, and these physicians do not know anything about what can be done by a hygienic and dietetic treatment—by allowing nature to take care of the disease without throwing any obstructive treatment in her way.

Uncleanliness plays a great part in this disease. Many men and women have hydrophobia so far as real cleanliness is concerned. A chancre makes an ideal breeding place for germs. Filth always favors decomposition. Is it any wonder that abraded surfaces easily become the site of infection? It is said that negroes are more easily infected than any other race, because they are not cleanly. It is doubtful if uncleanliness is a racial distinction. If the claim is true that the Jews suffer less than the Gentiles, it is probably due to the fact that circumcision removes a natural receptacle for the retention of decomposing secretions.

All careful observers have noticed that syphilis runs a more severe course in those afflicted with tuberculosis, Bright's disease or any of the other diseases of debility. This is not only true of syphilis, but of any other infection. Those who have broken down their resistance readily become victims to any disease influence, and the manner of manifestation will depend on the constitution, environment and the location of the exciting cause. It may be syphilis and it may be pneumonia. Hence, we can truthfully say that anything that breaks down an individual's resistance is a contributory cause of syphilis.

People who are suffering from severe forms of autointoxication are as susceptible to infection as dry grass is to an ignited match. In both cases there will be a rapid spread of the destructive process immediately upon exposure. The amount of infection that will kill a person in this physical state will fail to make an impression on those who are healthy.

This is true of the influence of the disease called syphilis. Those who keep themselves in a wholesome physical state are able to resist the infective process or, in other words, will not generate the infection, while those who abuse themselves until their resisting power is gone fall ready victims. Of course, after the disease is once established the subsequent course depends upon the treatment. Those who would have their cure spread over two or three years with an uncertain ending need only to have the "specific" treatment.

Those who carry decomposing material in their bowels take on syphilis easily and it runs a severe course in these subjects.

Constipation and its causes must be looked after and got rid of as soon as possible; otherwise, any and all infections spread rapidly.

Another complication is a too liberal indulgence in alcoholics. The overindulgence of one's appetites and passions in any and all directions is predisposed to intensify this disease, as it does all others.

If one would avoid syphilis, it is necessary to live correctly and keep wholesome and clean. Those who practice right living will not fall into habits of excess to which the sufferers from syphilis are generally inclined.

There are people whose lives are made burdensome because they fear this disease; they have been made to believe that they are liable to contract infection in many ridiculously impossible and improbable ways; they are phobic on the subject. This is a form of insanity that requires both physical and mental education. I hope to show before I get through with the subject that the treatment sanctioned by the regular profession is more to be feared than the disease.

# CHAPTER IV.

---

## PATHOLOGY.

---

HE PATHOLOGY and symptomatology of syphilis are so closely related that it is almost impossible to write of one without touching upon the other. ;

Syphilis is said to be the clown of diseases; it is a dissembler; it is more versatile than any protean actor; it is more varied and variegated than Joseph's coat; its skin manifestations simulate, in different subjects, nearly all cutaneous disorders known.

The reason for this supposed variation is because syphilis is not a specific disease. It must vary as individuals, secretions, habits and treatment vary.

It is without doubt a disease that thrives best in constitutions that show a decided tendency to develop an acid state of the secretions. This is the worst possible type in which to administer mercury, and this accounts for the havoc wrought in many cases. The skin, mucous-membrane and bone lesions are built by mercury and not by the so-called syphilis.

Local lesions in a subject giving a normal reaction to his secretions and excretions will not become infected.

It would require great professional skill to develop such a case ideally, and by ideally I mean in a way to conform to textbook descriptions. People who are much broken in health from excesses and improper living can have many marked symptoms without being under medical advice, but it will fail to act as the text-books say it should.

Several hundred years ago a query to the following effect was propounded: "How much of the process comes from the disease itself and how much from the treatment?" No doubt the one who asked the question was silenced by the contempt of his be-whiskered brethren.

In Professor Morrow's voluminous book one of the con-tributors speculates in regard to the existence of syphilis in ancient times. He inclines to the opinion that it existed in the prehistoric period. He says: "Should not the bones of a prehistoric race, where no efficient treatment interposed a barrier against the en-croachment of the disease, exhibit in an intense degree, if such a disease had prevailed when the race yet survived, the osseous lesions of syphilis? It is almost true that the reverse is the rule."

Of course the reverse is the rule. It is always true that the more obstructive treatment a sick man is forced to undergo the more pathology there is. In prehistoric times we can not say exactly what was done by our ancestors for their ills, but we are perfectly safe in asserting that complex compounds of iodine and mercury were not given. Perhaps they were fortunate enough to have no drug healers.

One of the most favorable diseases for demonstrating that the doctor is the chief builder of pathology is typhoid fever. The more "heroic" the treatment the more severe the disease. It is only those who treat the fever a great deal and keep up the patient's strength till he dies of degenerative changes, toxemia and exhaus-tion who have the privilege of performing post mortems and de-scribing the extensive ulcerations of the intestines, the degeneration

of the heart and other muscles, the inflammations of the bones,
mucous and serous membranes.   The physicians who allow their
patients complete rest in every way do not increase the pathology,
and consequently they do not have enough cases presenting typical
symptoms and dying to become expert pathologists.   This is a loss
to medical science!   But let us hope that the lives saved are of
sufficient value to compensate in an economic way, inasmuch as the
slogan of regular medicine is "vital economy."

It is the same in syphilis.   The doctors have been building
pathology for years, and this has resulted in symptoms so numerous
and fantastic that they even astonish and confuse those who build
them.

If this disease did not have a stigma attached to it by popular
opinion, and if it did not cause so many people physical and
mental suffering, it would be amusing to watch it when treated
by one of our eminent specialists, one of the ethical variety, not a
newspaper advertiser.   All he does is to use mercury and iodide
of potassium, with which he can produce for exhibition pustules,
discolorations, papules, ulcers, gummata, cicatrices, strictures, and
that isn't all.

The symptoms and pathology described are not necessary,
but they show what medical art can accomplish in building disease.   If nature unaided produced the text-book pathology we
would be forced to believe that chaos reigns supreme when
syphilis is at the helm, but as most of the symptoms are protests
made by nature against meddlesome treatment, such conclusions
are not justified.   It is well to bear in mind that a great deal of
what follows is doctor made.

For convenience of description this disease is divided into
three stages—primary, secondary and tertiary.   This is mislead-

ing, unless one bears in mind that there really are no well-defined stages; but that one stage gradually merges into another, without a line of demarcation.

The first stage is characterized by the formation of a chancre. This is an induration following a local irritation. The irritation produces inflammation, which results in what is termed the initial lesion, or chancre.

An inflammatory process is the same in its essentials wherever located. Since the ancient days and the fathers of medicine inflammation has been described the same; it is characterized by heat, pain, redness and swelling; to make the description more complete it is necessary to add that there is also an exudation or pouring out of the serum of the blood and more or less complete loss of functioning.

The initial lesion, then, is the result of inflammation following an irritation, and, as in all inflammations, cells are thrown out of the blood stream into the surrounding tissues; and this exudate favors the proliferation of connective tissue and is the cause of the hardening named chancre. This process is well illustrated in the liver diseases of habitual drinkers of alcoholics, for there is first an enlargement due to hyperemia, which causes excessive connective tissue formation, the pressure from which impairs nutrition to the extent of superinducing atrophy or contraction of the liver, which interferes with the circulation of the blood and the secretion of bile.

Where the local inflammation is severe the exudates are thrown into the coats of the arteries and surrounding tissues to such an extent that the arteries are obstructed. This cuts off nutrition, following which there is a breaking down or ulcerating of the chancre, and if the process is extensive it is called malignant or phagedenic. This takes place only in those subjects who are in such toxemic states that any disease influence is liable to end in destructive lesions or death, or in those who are subjected to a cauterizing local treatment that aggravates and extends the inflammation.

The throwing out of the exudate that ends in induration or chancre is a conservative measure. It is a barricade for keeping the toxic materials from gaining entrance into the circulation. But it often fails, for in spite of all resistance there is sufficient absorption to set up enough septic lymphangitis to infect the whole system. These glands are a part of the body's defense against disease, and when the poison reaches them they immediately begin to enlarge, which is meant to check by throwing out exudates; the result is that the glands become large and hard, the first ones affected are those of the groin; these enlargements are called buboes.

In the individual of average health this should end the trouble, and would if he were not improperly treated and if the correct mode of living were substituted for bad habits. But we are not dealing with conditions as they should be, but as they are; hence it is necessary to proceed with further ills. The subjects who are "regularly" treated are troubled with many annoying symptoms. They are morose and despondent; they do not sleep well; they do not relish their food, which they think is a great calamity, when in reality it is a hint that they should stop eating. Headaches are quite common, being more severe at night, and there are pains and aches all over the body, which are referred to at times as rheumatic pains. The syphilitic fever is often present, generally not very severe, but at times it is said to run up to 104°

F. This is an indication of an intercurrent affection or that the body is being unusually poisoned by the infection.

After a variable period what the individual fears most occurs—the skin eruptions advertise the subject's disease to those who have eyes and see. Many are fortunate enough to have their eruptions so situated that the clothes cover them. The worst punishment about the average case of syphilis is not so much in having the disease as in having it found out.

When the skin eruptions appear it is called the second stage. These eruptions are also the result of inflammation. The mildest form is the erythema, which is a mere blush that disappears upon pressure; this is followed by an eruption, which is in the form of irregular discolored spots. When these eruptions heal they leave a discoloration, which is supposed to be due to blood degeneration; the pigment, or brownish, coppery discoloration, is considered characteristic of the disease.

The papular eruption is more advanced than the other forms mentioned; the little nodules are exudates thrown out in the skin. Pustular eruptions take place in those who are in bad physical condition. Here small abscesses are formed in the skin.

The four varieties given above are the most common of the cutaneous disorders present in syphilis. They all result from the same process, namely, the inflammation followed by degeneration. They do not differ in kind, merely in degree. In erythema the degeneration is so slight that the products of the disease are easily absorbed by the circulatory system, while in pustular syphilis there is so much tissue destruction at times that ulcers form. Please keep in mind that drugs are necessary if a typical disease is to develop.

It is well to remember that the skin trouble is an index of degenerative changes taking place throughout the system. Wherever there is a point of irritation there is a favorable place for inflammation to take place, and the severity depends upon the strength of the toxic material and the resistance of the individual. This is true when not directly due to drugs.

The rupial syphilide is a peculiar lesion. It often starts from a pustule; a crust is formed by the drying of the secretions, and this adheres to the sore; other crusts are successively formed underneath, pushing the upper ones outward until there is a horn-like formation.

The lymphatic glands of the entire body become enlarged, showing that the intoxication is systemic.

One annoying feature is the temporary loss of hair, which is oftener caused by the so-called blood medicines than from the so-called specific disease. The scalp is one part usually affected. The baldness may occur in spots, syphilitic alopecia areata.

During the continuation of the symptoms enumerated above the mental condition is bad. These patients worry for fear others will find out about their trouble; they consider themselves disgraced. The average young man does not want any of the members of the family to know his condition. Worry and evasion are in themselves enough to bring on bad health.

The third stage is not present in the majority of cases. The medical profession assumes the credit of preventing this. The doctors claim that their mercurial treatment cures the disease before it advances to this stage. However, text-book syphilis is very treacherous, and it may be two years or it may be twenty years after the patient has been cured with mercury before there are any tertiary manifestations. In this stage there are none of the early symptoms. The symptoms of the third stage may vary from a gummatous tumor in the brain to some degenerative change in one of the feet.

Volumes have been written on tertiary syphilis, authors taking up the different anatomical structures and describing their pathology separately, detailing the pathological changes and symptoms resulting in each; but this is not necessary, for a gumma in the brain is essentially the same as one in the liver. Wherever a gumma appears it is the result of inflammation. Cells of less stability than those of the tissues where they are formed lodge in the connective tissue; these cells are sometimes called embryonic; they become the nucleus around which gather a deposit, and it is called a gummatous tumor.

The instability of the cellular elements causes gummata to degenerate easily. Sometimes inflammation ensues, followed by liquefaction of the deposited substance; at other times the deposit takes on caseatious degeneration; again, it may end in fatty degeneration or suppuration. Sometimes the gumma is simply absorbed when metabolism becomes normal. Where there is enough inflammation present to close the lumen of the blood vessels (endarteritis obliterans) some form of degeneration always ensues.

To sum up, the third stage of syphilis means those extensive retrograde changes which take place in the deep tissues of those who have suffered from the primary and secondary forms; the most characteristic change is that of the formation of gummata.

The symptoms depend upon the seat of the lesion and its size. A gumma in the motor area of the brain would cause paralysis, if it caused any trouble at all, while one in the aorta might produce an aneurysm. Some of the after effects of syphilitic degeneration are not only annoying, but serious. The uvula may be destroyed. The nasal septum may be ulcerated away, causing facial disfigurement. The organs of speech may be destroyed by ulceration, and there may be contractions of any of the hollow organs of the body, such as the esophagus or any part of the bowel. This list could be extended for pages; but the most important point to make is that these pathological manifestations are absolutely unnecessary.

Surely the medical profession should feel proud of its ability and power in creating so destructive a disease. By the aid of a few drugs they are able to conjure up conditions such as nature alone has never equaled, at least such as competent observers have never seen her equal in devilish grotesqueness when left to herself.

The tendency of late years is to blame syphilis for more and more of the nervous disorders from which people suffer. Some medical men claim that this disease causes all cases of locomotor ataxia. It is true that many of the ataxics have had syphilis, but by no means all of them. Many of them have also had measles and corns. Locomotor ataxia has as varied a causation as other diseases have, and to blame some previous disorder is either mental laziness or perversion of the truth.

*Diagnosis.*—On account of the multiplicity of its lesions and the variability of its manifestations syphilis is at times hard to diagnose; so much of it is the handiwork of man, and, like the description of man that is taught us in another branch of knowledge, it, too, is fearfully and wonderfully made, so much so that it is hard to recognize. This is especially true when no primary lesion can be found and when there is no history of one. A positive history of a primary sore, followed by the train of symptoms and pathological manifestations described above, would establish a diagnosis, but all cases are not typical.

Some diagnose by exclusion; that is, they try out the case in hand with every other known disease, and if the symptoms fail to agree with all other diseases they can think of, it must be syphilis. To diagnose in this way requires more knowledge than most of the best doctors possess.

Of late years we have had the advantage of a scientific procedure, the Wassermann test. If trying out this test is not interesting and instructive, it should be, for some of the most capable men in the profession are wasting their time experimenting with it. A brilliant man can put as much time and energy into a useless task as he can into a task that will prove of benefit to humanity. It seems to be largely a matter of being started in the right or wrong direction, for very few people have the power of being original and logical at the same time. Those who are doing speculative laboratory work and others who are performing unnecessary surgical operations are honored beyond all others in the profession. It seems that the more fantastic and useless their theories and practice and the results following the more praise and glory they get.

To make a Wassermann reaction is quite a feat. The following quotation from The Practical Medicine Series gives but a faint idea of what is necessary, yet this is a simplification of the original method:

Physiologic salt solution, prepared by dissolving one salt tablet in 12 c. c. of water.

Antigen (alcoholic organ extract).

Complement (guinea-pig serum, dried upon filter paper).

Amboceptor (hemolytic immune serum prepared against human red corpuscles).

Patient's serum.

Emulsion of human red cells (obtained by collecting 10 or 12 drops of blood from the patient, transferring it to the defibrinator and shaking vigorously until filaments of fibrin are seen attached to the beads).

These are some of the things necessary to make the test; it is necessary to have about a dozen test tubes and make various mixtures with the patient's blood. If there is a settling of the red corpuscle elements in the bottom of the tube the reaction is positive, and indicates that the disease is present.

This would be all right if it were trustworthy, but it is not. The diagnostician is just where he started, for if he is honest he can only say this positively after the test has been made, "Perhaps you have it and perhaps you haven't." It requires skill and time to make the test, and the one examined is no better off than before, while the doctor is generally ahead to the tune of a few dollars.

This is scientific medicine and a recognized procedure. If it helped to bring about a better understanding of the disease there could be no objection to it, but after a positive reaction is obtained the doctors know of nothing to do except to give mercury, or, if truly up to date, salvarsan. To show how dependable this test is I give extracts from The Practical Medicine Series:

J. E. R. McDonough says that a positive reaction can be obtained in only 40 per cent. of primary cases, and that no reliance should be placed upon a negative Wassermann reaction in the primary stage. In the secondary stage a positive result occurs in 85 per cent. of cases, whether eruption be present, or even when no manifestation of the lesion exists, and when the patient is undergoing treatment.

In the tertiary stage 70 per cent. give a positive result.

The usual errors are evident in the absolute claims made for the diagnostic powers of the serum in face of the facts that the reaction occurs in scarlatina, in pellagra, in Hodgkin's disease, in leprosy, and in a number of other states, and does not always occur in syphilis. Of the influence of medication upon it very contradictory reports are rendered. The most accurately made and analyzed tend to show that iodin, arsenic and mercury affect it.

Of course, the finding of the spirocheta pallida is considered proof positive that the disease is in the system. But the spirocheta pallida is hard to find, and there are other spirilla that resemble it closely. One trouble with the microscope is that one is liable to find what he is searching for, even if it is not present; as the Bible says, "Search and ye shall find."

Another method of diagnosis that has been in vogue for years is fully as good as any of the above, and fully as sensible. It is the therapeutic test. If the doctor has any suspicion that he is dealing with syphilis he gives mercury. If the patient gets well he had syphilis; if he does not respond it is some other trouble. All this is called medical science, and a part of it is modern medicine.

In spite of scientific refinement, the best method of diagnosing the trouble is to examine and observe the patient.

# CHAPTER V.

---

## TREATMENT.

---

EFORE giving the treatment of this disease it will be well to preface it with a cursory history of mercury. For over 400 years this metal has been the principal remedy used in the treatment of syphilis, and in spite of the harm it has done the medical profession is as firmly wedded to it as ever.

It now seems that another harmful remedy, Prof. Ehrlich's alleged specific, salvarsan or "606," is to be foisted upon a not too discriminating public. In fact, this compound has already secured a strong hold on professional, as well as lay, imagination, not from merit, but because it had such a scientific backing! Four hundred years from now we shall probably have had many other like specifics discovered, and syphilis will not have abdicated unless man has learned to stay clean inside as well as outside.

Mercury had a fascination for the ancients on account of its peculiar form. The Romans called it liquid silver (hydrargyrum) and the alchemists spent much time working with it trying to make it, one of the base elements, precious!

When an epidemic of syphilis spread over Europe in the last part of the 15th century, is it any wonder that the physicians, not knowing what to do, turned to this wonderful substance with its witchery and charmlike appearance? It was easier to obtain than dragon's blood or ground criminal's skull. Its use has spread until it is now the approved remedy in every civilized country; a fact that is a grotesque travesty in the face of so much boasted advance.

It was not used with the scientific refinement that it is used today. The doctors believed in heroic treatment in those days.

Mercury was at one time the chief remedy in all kinds of fevers. In the "good old days," nearly everybody believed in hell, and if we do not misjudge, the physicians tried to give their fever patients a taste of it while they were still on earth. The usual mode of treatment was to put them into a close room, one without windows preferred; then shut all the doors, raise the temperature by means of artificial heat, and give mercury to the point of salivation. The patient was put to bed and clothes piled on him. This produced profuse perspiration. To accelerate the cure water was withheld. The teeth might fall out and the bones ulcerate, but the treatment was a success. In comparison with the tortures of the inquisition, this treatment was not so bad.

Mercury gives rise to two lines of salts, the higher being called mercuric, of which the bichloride or corrosive sublimate (hydrargyri chloridum corrosivum) is a representative. The mercuric salts are freely soluble and poisonous. Bichloride is the most powerful all-round antiseptic known. The advocates of its internal use say that a 1 to 1000 solution will sterilize any like amount of morbid material, which is true enough. It should not be forgotten that sterilization is a killing process and that if enough of the remedy is given to a patient to kill the germs in his system it will kill the patient without a doubt. If enough is given to slowly poison the germs, it will cause degeneration and slow poisoning of the patient as well.

The second or lower line of mercurial salts is called mercurous, of which mercurous chloride or calomel is the most used and best known. The mercurous salts are comparatively inert and insoluble. However, medical literature records deaths due to the use of calomel. In such cases it is likely that a sufficient amount has been converted into the poisonous bichloride or oxide to cause death. Calomel is used a great deal to stimulate liver and bowel action, so it is as well to know that, although it, as a rule, does no apparent harm, it has produced constitutional mercurial poisoning and death. If it acts quickly it is evacuated by the bowel movement, but if conditions are favorable for its conversion into soluble salts, absorption takes place with constitutional mercurialization.

An overdose of a number of the mercuric salts, including the bichloride, causes acute poisoning. They are caustic and corrosive, producing ulceration of the tissues they touch; if the esophagus and stomach are burned very severely, death ensues in a time varying from less than an hour to several days. The symptoms are the same as in poisoning by other caustics.

A more interesting phase is the mercurial poisoning produced by continued use of the drug. This is the sort found in those who have undergone the popular treatment for syphilis, for it is nothing more than systemic mercurialization. The poisoning can be either chronic or acute.

In cases of poisoning by mercury there is a peculiar metallic taste in the mouth, the saliva becomes profuse and tenacious, the teeth sensitive, the gums inflame, and at first they are light in

color and then they become red and spongy.  If the mercury is
continued the teeth become loose and even drop out, the tongue
and parotid glands swell, and ulcers form on the mucous membranes of the mouth and throat.

The condition of the mouth and throat is an index to the
condition to be found on the mucous membrane of the stomach
and bowels.  It is not to be wondered at that people suffering
from such treatment lose appetite, become weak, depressed and
nervous, have indigestion, gastro-intestinal catarrh, headaches and
other symptoms too variable and numerous to mention.

Of course, such severe types of malpractice are extremely
rare now; people would not tolerate the abuse, but a number
of years ago salivation was very common and intentional.  Such
treatment is worse than the disease.  Cases are recorded where
mercury caused destruction of the jaw bones, and if it can destroy
the jaw bone why not the shin bone, or any other bone in the body,
or the soft tissue?  Most doctors of extensive practice have observed victims of this practice in whom bone ulceration was extensive, requiring a surgical operation to remove the dead bone.

The abuse of mercury and blood-letting was a strong factor
in causing the medical discontent during the early part of the
19th century which resulted in the formation of the Eclectic
School of medicine.  During the infancy of this school its members strongly opposed the use of mercury in any form, but they
have not discovered a remedy for syphilis that has given universal
satisfaction to the school as a body; consequently they are re-
sorting more and more to mercury as a specific.  So great is the
influence of authority that the ordinary physician would rather
be wrong and popular, than be right and ostracised.  It takes

too much time and effort to maintain unpopular views; it requires too much fighting for one's opinions.

One of the towering figures among the early Eclectics was Prof. John King. He was a chemist, a physician, a gentleman and a scholar. His explanation of the action of mercury is the best I have seen, although it was penned 65 years ago. The following paragraphs are taken from an article written by Dr. King in 1846 and reprinted in the March number of "The Gleaner":

In the form of an oxide, then, is mercury carried into the mass of blood, to be thence circulated to every part of the system. Combining with the phosphoric acid of the bones, a phosphate of mercury is formed, leaving the bone in the state of an oxide of calcium, or common lime; the bony structure being thus chemically decomposed, crumbles and exfoliates.

A similar combination with the phosphoric acid of the nerves and brain produces nervousness, severe pains, loss of memory, headache, etc., and as the changes of the atmosphere act upon mercury in any state, the suffering patient can predict the various changes about to take place in the weather, with as much precision as could be derived from the most delicate barometer.

The oxide of mercury is capable of producing decomposition to some extent in every fluid or solid of the human body. And if any gentleman of the old school can disprove the above explanation of the modus operandi of mercury, I trust you will allow him the use of the columns of your journal, that is, if he dares to risk his reputation, or expose his ignorance, by attempting it.

It is claimed that mercury in moderate doses is a tonic and has a very beneficial effect upon the nutrition. This is as absurd as thousands of other therapeutic claims.

That mercury is an agent causing tissue degeneration cannot be successfully disputed. Everyone knows its effects on the mouth and teeth.

Mercury does not belong in the body; it is not a constituent of the tissues. It is a foreign agent and when absorbed into the body it is an irritant. The system eliminates it to a certain extent. However, the evidence points to the fact that it remains in the system indefinitely. Some clinicians claim that it is all expelled in six months; others say in a year; but when we remember that nearly all therapeutic science is nothing more than guess work or bombastic assertion, this statement need not be taken very seriously. If, for the sake of argument, this statement be accepted as true, why do people who have been thoroughly mercurialized become as sensitive to weather changes as a barometer, and why do they remain in this state indefinitely? The correct answer is, probably some of the mercury remains in the body for life, and produces a permanent detrimental effect

We hear much prating about the curative action of this and that remedy upon the body, but cures are not forthcoming in proof of these contentions. If a drug causes a chemical change in the body, assimilation is interfered with until the intruder is treated as a foreign substance and expelled when possible. Calomel is an irritant and causes the intestinal glands to secrete more than they do normally, and the muscles in the walls of the intestines to contract more vigorously, and this is why it is often given as a physic. Drugs have no eliminative action, but because they have a local irritating effect they cause the body to overwork to expel them. Such drug action is on the order of a cinder in the eye or a thorn in the flesh. The action is very stimulating but the result is depressing. A cinder in the eye is fully as beneficial as the average stimulant used to increase the various physiological processes of the body.

The different ways of administering mercury have received much attention and aroused much contention. Some advocate the use of a soluble salt hypodermically; others declare that rubbing it into the skin in the form of ointment is the correct method. Another method is to vaporize mercury and have it settle on the skin; then there are mercurial baths. The most common method is to give it internally; but in this, as usual, doctors disagree. Some declare that the hypodermic method is the best, while others are as positive that this plan of medication is dangerous.

Dr. J. W. White, in an article contributed to Dr. Morrow's book on syphilis, gives the following objections to the hypodermatic method:

It is painful, and in many patients excites apprehension and is strongly objected to. It might be added that the measures advocated to obviate or lessen pain, viz., the precedent or simultaneous administration of morphia or cocaine, are in themselves highly objectionable and certainly ought to be discouraged.

It is occasionally though rarely dangerous, and sometimes rapidly fatal.

It is liable to be followed by certain local complications which are (a) erythema; (b) painful nodosities; (c) cellulitis; (d) abscess; (e) sloughing

Dr. White's criticism is not unique; text-books vie with each other in condemning treatment not their own. He fails, however, as do all medicators, to make the proper objection, namely, that mercury is bad in any form. He believes in giving it by mouth and inunction.

According to this authority, mercury given by the hypodermic method causes erythema, nodosities, cellulitis, abscess and sloughing. Why cannot he see that it will do the same when given by mouth? It is merely a matter of getting it into the blood; it is not always absorbed when given by mouth. The hypodermic injection (usually of bichloride) is liable to be followed

by one of the lesions enumerated at or near the site of the injection, while mercury when taken into the stomach, even if absorbed, will not necessarily be followed by any of these local
lesions, for its action may be confined to the hidden structures of
the body.

A mercurial erythema, or inflammation of the surface of the
body, following inunction is not uncommon, and sometimes this
inflammation is very severe. It is due to the fact that the soluble
mercurial salts are very irritating, even corroding to the skin and
mucous membrane of some people.

Irritation, inflammation, degeneration and death are all parts
of the same process, and the extent of the process depends on the
amount of the drug absorbed, and this depends on the amount of
vital resistance of the patient.

Mercury is an agent causing general physical and mental
degeneration; the more that is absorbed the more liable the
subject is to have mental perversions, abscesses and sloughs.

Iodin is the second remedy in importance employed in the
treatment of syphilis. Potassium and sodium iodides are the salts
generally used. The iodin salts are very irritating. Their use
very soon upsets the stomach; when a victim of syphilis has indigestion it is very hard for medicators to do anything for him
with this drug until the stomach is better. Nearly all drugs used
in the treatment of this disease are inclined to cause gastro-
intestinal irritation, which, at least, means indigestion.

Iodin taken internally causes cutaneous disorders, ranging
from a mild erythema to pustules. In fact, it would be hard to
think of many skin diseases that are not simulated by the erup-

tions caused by iodides. Even the severe inflammation known as purpura sometimes results from the ingestion of this drug.

There is a chance for some good nomenclator to do good service classifying the eruptions caused by the treatment of syphilis, so that doctors may know the types caused by mercury, by the iodides and by uncomplicated syphilis. This would prove conclusively to what extent drugs complicate. It is our belief that the symptoms are due more to the treatment than to the disease.

Besides causing gastro-intestinal irritation and skin eruptions the iodides cause rhinitis, in fact, inflammation of all mucous membranes, nervousness and depression, ringing in the ears, and lachrymation. It is well to remember that the skin is one of the most resistant organs of the body and whatever remedy is powerful enough to cause purpura and pustules will do injury to the rest of the body.

It may be asked why spend so much time on mercury when salvarsan is to be the remedy of the future? The answer is because doctors are already losing their enthusiasm and beginning to desert the new remedy, and of course this means that they will go back to mercury and iodin again.

# CHAPTER VI.

---

## SALVARSAN IN SYPHILIS.

---

ARSENIC is an intensely irritating poison. Any of its soluble salts or compounds have the power of quickly destroying life, even in doses of two or three grains. A large dose causes acute arsenical poisoning, the symptoms being much the same as in poisoning by other irritants.

If arsenic is taken into the system in small but repeated doses it will bring on fatty degeneration of various structures, such as the liver, the glands and the muscles of the body. Fatty degeneration of the heart is one of the most dangerous sequels.

This may account for many of the sudden deaths from *heart failure.*

It is no uncommon thing for physicians to give Fowler's Solution and arsenical triturations for chronic malaria, syphilis, and physical depression from other causes. When given for such diseases, it is continued for weeks and sometimes for months, and as the drug is cumulative, in the course of time arsenical poisoning will result, be the dose administered ever so small.

A peculiarity of arsenic is that it disturbs the vision; sometimes it is nothing more than a temporary functional derangement, while at other times complete blindness ensues. If it causes atrophy of the optic nerve the blindness will be permanent.

It is reasonable to believe that a remedy that affects the optic nerves in this way also has a deleterious effect on the rest of the nervous system.

Dr. Koch (of tuberculin fame) treated over 1,600 individuals for sleeping sickness with arsenic; twenty-two of these became permanently blind.

Professor Ehrlich, who is responsible for the introduction of salvarsan, claims that his patent medicine will not cause blindness; that where the blindness follows the use of the drug it is due to syphilis, not to salvarsan. This is merely begging the question, and will not convince those who have studied the action of arsenic. The professor is simply prejudiced in his own favor.

Salvarsan, "606," or arsenobenzol is being tried out in many different forms of diseases. In malaria it has been found excellent in some cases, while others have become worse under its influence. In anemia it is much better than Fowler's Solution, a comparison quite without meaning, for it assumes that Fowler's Solution is remedial for anemia, which is a medical delusion.

It is said to be of doubtful use in pellagra, but a specific for frambesia. As this is a disease confined to the tropics, most of us will have to take science's word for it.

Subconsciously the medical profession feels its inability to cure; that is why it seizes upon every new discovery as a life-saver. If an eminent chemist like Ehrlich should bottle up some ditch water and recommend it highly, it would be thought to produce many cures in the hands of enthusiastic doctors.

Professor Ehrlich enjoys as high esteem in Germany as Koch ever did. His laboratory work and his theory regarding immunity are known to medical men of all countries. For this reason any remedy he introduces will receive respectful attention.

During his researches he discovered that the tissue stains he used did not color all tissues alike. For instance, methylene blue stains the nerves more deeply than other tissues. From these observations he reasoned that each kind of disease germ has an affinity for a certain remedy. All that is necessary is to discover and apply the remedy and the disease will be overcome, for, he reasons, the remedy kills the germs. This form of therapeutics has been given the pretentious name of therapia sterilisans magna. The fact that any remedy that is powerful enough to kill the micro-organisms in the body is also powerful enough to kill the body has been consistently and persistently overlooked.

The probable mistake made by those who believe in sterilizing the blood and tissues of the body is that all immune animals are possessed of antibodies and all diseased animals are deficient in these bodies; therefore, artificial immunization must be a logical remedy. This is not true, for the former process is physiological and the latter is chemical.

The dispute has been on among physicians since drugs have been used in the treatment of disease. Some contend for a chemical food and remedy while others contend for a physiological food and remedy. The former believe disease can be cured by chemicals, while the latter believe such treatment at most is only palliative and, in fact, no remedy at all.

In the January, 1911, CLUB Dr. Tilden predicted that the profession would soon wake up to the fact that it had been fooled again. At that time there was nothing but praise for the new remedy, but now, May, 1911, that salvarsan has rendered some blind and killed others, a warning note is creeping into all literature on the subject.

The fact of the matter is that Ehrlich has attempted the impossible. There is no such thing as vicarious atonement in the plan of nature. Disease must be removed by getting rid of the cause. An injection of arsenic or morphine; an inunction of mercury, or a dose of digitalis, never cured anything; many drugs are, however, capable of producing temporary relief. That is all people ask for, and that is all the profession has given, notwithstanding each time a doctor relieves a patient he calls it a cure.

Quite a number have told me of remarkable cures made by the use of this drug, and have asked me to explain. It is never safe to draw conclusions from the apparent results in one case. In the first place the doctors who use salvarsan have been hoodwinked into believing that it is a specific. They have instilled their belief and faith into their patients. It is a positive fact that faith and renewed hope will cause an improvement in 100 per cent. of all sick people, even if nothing is done for them. Besides this, arsenic is a stimulant and has a temporary toning-up effect, but the effect is strictly temporary.

Salvarsan was introduced with timbrel, cymbals and dancing. Medical men pointed with pride to its advent. They declared they had a remedy that would conquer a disease which for hundreds of years had defied their skill, notwithstanding that this disease is about the only one for which they have had a specific.

Whether the doctors believe it or not, they have allowed the impression to become public that salvarsan is a specific. I wonder if the medical profession will ask all the newspapers who published laudatory articles to explain to their readers that the statements were premature; that salvarsan is a dangerous, even a deadly drug. Perhaps the popular magazines that told in glowing terms what wonders this drug performs will do likewise! They certainly ought to, for such articles as they published are misleading to their readers.

According to the American Journal of the Medical Sciences, which is one of the oldest and, in my estimation, the best of the orthodox medical journals published in this country, salvarsan should not be given when the individual is seriously ill:

"Ehrlich says that from the first he has given as contraindications for salvarsan treatment those patients with irritable hearts due to nervous causes, organic heart disease, vascular degenerations, aneurysms, old cases of cerebral hemorrhage, and the aged. He now adds to this list the following: Serious nephritis, diabetes, and ulcer of the stomach. He does not consider the remedy a harmless one, but one that should be used with caution in properly selected cases."

It is well to note how exceedingly tactful the profession is when it comes to introducing a new remedy. They do not burn all bridges behind them; instead, they construct more bridges over which they may beat a hasty though dignified retreat. If th remedy fails to work, the excuse is that it was not used in properly selected cases; while, if the patient gets well, all credit is due to the drug and none to nature.

If one eliminates the more serious cases there should be no difficulty in treating the rest. A specific should cure all cases; otherwise it is not worthy of the name.

The following are quotations from the same journal:

"So far as the results may be taken into consideration as evidence of a cure of the disease, if we accept a positive Wassermann reaction as evidence of the continued presence of the so-called specific virus in the system, we must conclude that salvarsan does not cure syphilis even though it may clear up the symptoms of the disease."

"One child, eight days old, showed lesions of congenital syphilis on its body and had visceral lues at birth. The mother showed no syphilitic signs. The Wassermann reaction was positive in both mother and child. The general condition of the child was poor and the prognosis bad. In the second case the infant developed a syphilitic eruption shortly after birth and had 'snuffles,' but its general condition and prognosis were good. The Wassermann reaction was positive in mother and child. In both infants, after their mothers were injected with '606,' the lesion and the syphilitic conditions were somewhat improved, but shortly became worse and both children died."

"Our first and only case injected with salvarsan intravenously died two weeks after the injection of acute mania. Unfortunately an autopsy could not be obtained, and we are at a loss for an explanation of the cause of death. Inasmuch as there were no manifest symptoms of arsenical poisoning, and in view of the fact that the patient was addicted to the excessive use of alcohol (he had been on a spree five days after the injection of the drug, immediately preceding his re-admission to the hospital in an irrational condition), we are loth to ascribe the fatal issue to the drug."

The Wassermann reaction is considered diagnostic, yet a positive reaction persists in spite of the use of salvarsan. However, the Wassermann reaction is no more reliable than the therapeutic measures that have been used in connection with syphilis. One worker along these lines stated that if the reaction is positive, syphilis is present, but if it is negative that does not signify the absence of the disease. In some the reaction may change two or three times inside of two months. Of what value is a test of this kind? It is simply a waste of the doctor's time and the patient's money, so far as any real benefit is concerned.

A death rate of two children out of two treated ought to satisfy even the most exacting. The fact of the matter is, that children are very susceptible to poisons, and it does not take a great deal to produce death.

Of course, the drunkard may have died from over-indulgence in liquor, or from exposure, or from both of these causes, or he may have died from the effects of the arsenic, or the arsenic may have been only a contributory factor. There is a strong tendency to give the drug the benefit of the doubt. This is not as it should be when one is dealing with deadly therapeutic agents. The individual should be given the benefit of the doubt, for his life is at stake.

The following quotations are all taken from the Journal of the American Medical Association. It should be borne in mind that all the extracts quoted in this article are taken from papers written by men who believe in the salvarsan treatment, and published in journals that favor this form of therapy.

"In two cases of optic neuritis a temporary arrest in the progress of the affection was noted, but subsequently the disease pursued its course to complete blindness."

"A robust peasant girl of 19; infection 8 weeks old; multiple sclerosis and beginning roseola. August 2 she received 0.45 gm. neutral suspension intragluteally. The clinical manifestations disappeared quickly and by September 30 the Wassermann reaction was negative. October 5 she returned with headache, vertigo, visual disturbances, right-sided oculomotor paresis, beginning optic neuritis of the left eye; Wassermann again positive. Her condition was considered a recurrence, for which she was given October 12, 0.45 gm. in acid solution subcutaneously. October 28 she was placed on mercury and potassium iodid but without result, and neuritis of the right optic nerve set in."

It is necessary to repeat over and over again that drugs do not cure anything. People realize that drugs do not cure pneumonia, nor do they cure typhoid fever. Yet they think that possibly arsenic may be a curative agent in unusual diseases. It cures nothing, but it is irritating enough to cause inflammation of the optic nerve, and the process may be severe enough to end in optic nerve atrophy and blindness.

Here is reported a robust peasant girl, certainly a favorable case for a speedy and complete cure. Salvarsan is specific; it failed to cure. Mercury is specific; it failed to cure, even when reinforced by potassium iodid, which is considered almost specific. The profession really needs a few more specifics.

When will this comedy of errors cease? It seems that a young fellow who spends four years in college, absorbing nonsense and medical errors, is almost sure to have both his eyes and his mind closed to the truth.

If a few doctors were misled by German scientists it would not be cause for surprise, but when practically the whole profession runs after strange gods one is compelled to believe that no independent thinking is being done. Until the majority of medical men begin to think independently, and have the courage of their convictions, the profession will continue playing at doctoring with hypodermics, inunctions, internal medicine and surgery at the expense of the public.

"Rille states that recurrence has been observed in fourteen of the forty syphilitics kept under observation since treatment with salvarsan. He further reports three cases in which patients with recent infection developed severe symptoms on the part of the cranial nerves. In the first, deafness came on four weeks after the injection, facial paralysis two weeks later, and choked disc a week and a half later. The patient was a robust girl of 21. The second patient was likewise a previously healthy girl of 18, infected with syphilis about four months before the injection of the drug. Nearly eight weeks afterward headache and vertigo developed, followed three weeks later by right facial paralysis and after another week by bilateral optic neuritis and right fourth nerve paralysis. In the third case a blacksmith became deaf nearly thirteen weeks after the injection, given three months after primary infection. Only one of these patients had recovered entirely at date of writing. Rille adds that complications of this kind have never been observed after mercurial treatment, but he does not venture to decide whether they are manifestations of the Herxheimer reaction or the result of an especial affinity of the drug for the nerve tissue."

It would be interesting to know how many cases are treated for syphilis who do not have it at all. They are not few, for we see many of them. How do I know that they are not syphilitics? They get well without mercury, salvarsan or any other drug, which surely ought to be proof enough.

It is almost as bad for one to believe he has a disease as to really have it. In the past all good orthodox doctors have been in the habit of telling these people that it is necessary for them to undergo a course of treatment for two or three years. If business is slack and there is a prospect of a steady income from an individual for two or three years the temptation to diagnose syphilis is great. If lesions are present in any part of the body that are hard to account for and a history of a sore on the genitals can be elicited that is generally sufficient to establish a diagnosis of syphilis. In this way the disease is diagnosed in many who do not have it, but after they have undergone the regulation treatment for a while they might as well have had it.

It would indeed be peculiar if other nerves than the optic were not also affected. Why should not other nerves atrophy and become paralyzed? Arsenic acts more quickly and is more toxic than the mercurials, except when large doses of such active poisons as the bichloride are given.

The Herxheimer reaction, which is an exacerbation of the symptoms after the administration of a therapeutic agent, is merely a systemic objection to being poisoned.

"1. The medical profession should use every effort possible to eradicate the idea that appears to have become prevalent in the minds of the laity, and, indeed, of many of the profession, that a single dose of salvarsan will permanently cure syphilis.

"2. Salvarsan should be administered under the best scientific conditions possible, which means that no patient should be treated until they have been in a hospital four days and careful records made of their physical condition. Only patients in a healthy condition, aside from the syphilitic taint, should receive this form of treatment. Any attempt to treat patients when these precautions have not been taken, or any unscientific use of the preparation, should be strongly opposed by the profession, as these attempts are sure to result disastrously to the patient and also to detract from the merits of the remedy.

"3. Salvarsan is the treatment of election in the conditions of syphilis enumerated in this paper, but under all circumstances should be followed by mercury or the iodids, or both."

This is nothing but buncombe. It is written to confirm the professional brethren in the view that all the revenue from medical malpractice should flow into the pockets of the ethical brigands.

"Doblin gave salvarsan to six infants and reports that no benefit in the general condition of the child was observed in any instance, the children did not lose their pallor and did not increase in weight thereafter; one strong child died from salvarsan poisoning, although the dose was only 0.03 gm. In another case the infant gained 300 gm. in five days, which he regards as a sign of toxic action of the drug, like the herpes zoster sometimes observed in adults. Four of the infants died, including two in good condition before the injection; this was made subcutaneous or intramuscular in each case and there was little local reaction at the spot. The necropsy findings suggested, he reports, acute arsenic poisoning; acute paralysis of the central nervous system, coma, severe injury of the intestines with diarrhea, drop of the blood-pressure and total paralysis of the contractile elements of the mesenteric capillaries, the so-called splanchnic paralysis. The edema in the mesenteric and subcutaneous fat tissue was evidently the result of arsenic paralysis of the capillaries. The experiences related indicate, he thinks, that 0.03 gm. may be regarded as the fatal dose for infants under the age of 3 months. Even this amount does not ward off recurrence, and as improvement in the manifestations of the syphilis may be observed, as in one of his cases, even with so small an amount as 0.025 gm., it seems reasonable to accept for infants under 3 months from 0.01 to 0.02 gm. as the tolerated dosage, that is, 0.005 per kilogram of body weight."

At first it was thought that one dose of salvarsan would cure; now the fallacy of this is seen; perhaps it will be necessary to repeat as often as in mercurial therapeutics. It will probably have to be given till the arsenic causes fatty degeneration, optic nerve atrophy and death. With such a result everyone should be satisfied, for when the syphilitic dies the spirocheta pallida he has harbored soon die too, and the cure is complete; death is surely a gruesome climax for a treatment dignified by the name of therapia sterilisans magna.

Surely there is no one so blind to the beauties of medical experimentation that he will object to trying out poisonous remedies on children! Suppose four out of six die, are there not plenty of babies left! Perhaps the medical profession is weary of being attacked for being vivisectionists and animal experimenters, and now turn to baby experimentation. The profession has always experimented upon its patrons, but this fact has been hidden under the mask of professional duty.

The reports of infant mortality quoted in this article are taken from European sources. The American profession is aping the European profession more each year, and if this tendency continues it will not be long till American medical men will publish such reports without a blush. Physicians who have made the rounds of

German clinics accuse the German doctors of being more interested in postmortems than in the cure of their patients.

The use of salvarsan is not only dangerous, but at times produces intense pain lasting for days or even weeks and so severe that it requires morphine to control it.

# CHAPTER VII.

## TREATMENT OF SYPHILIS.

THE average individual is spared the trouble of preparing himself for being a good culture medium for disease. His parents usually attend to this for him from the time of his birth, and even before. During the gestation period mothers are told that they must eat enough for two. While this is very agreeable advice to most of them, and they follow it religiously, the result is that the offspring is overweight at birth.

After birth, the doctor, or someone else as badly misinformed, instructs the mother to feed the child every two hours, day and night. Under this forced feeding the mortality in children's diseases is made very great. Those children who do not die of diseases peculiar to teething, fall ready victims to diphtheria, measles, whooping-cough, scarlet fever and other diseases common to childhood. These disorders are symptoms of perverted nutrition due to overwork, notwithstanding doctors believe they have found the bacteria that cause some of them, and are on a still hunt for others, which they are quite sure will be discovered. These diseases are not necessary, and when treated conventionally there is great loss of life, besides there are left many children with health permanently impaired.

The continuation of the overfeeding habit causes various forms of irritations or chronic low-grade inflammations which often manifest themselves in adenoids and catarrh. The adenoids are "cured" by being cut out, but the catarrh on which they depend is not removed by the knife, and as the profession does nothing for it, it remains.

The stuffing habit is so persistently indulged in by every one that many do not know what feeling well really means. Their nutrition is so overtaxed that, in spite of long hours of sleep, they get up in the morning feeling tired, dull and heavy, and they remain in this condition all day because they persist in taking more food than they can digest and assimilate. The food decays —ferments in the stomach and bowels—some of the products of decomposition are absorbed, and the result is what is known as auto-intoxication.

These people carry dirty tongues, and their breaths are often offensive. They also have that large train of nervous symptoms which is due to the gas that comes from fermentation.

This is a physical state in which many people are doomed to remain through life. They are ready to succumb to any disease influence that prevails, and it is largely a matter of chance what disease they have. They suffer more severely and longer from any disease they happen to contract than do those who live more normal lives. The diseases they suffer have a tendency to take on a sthenic type, and they readily fall into septic states. The reason for this is that they have been preparing their blood for it for years, and all that is necessary to overcome their remaining resistance is an unusual infection. It does not make any difference whether the disease is considered respectable, as in the case of typhoid fever or pneumonia, or if it is one which it would be most unconventional to discuss at afternoon teas and other social functions, it runs a more severe course in these people.

Syphilis forms no exception to the general rule of cure. Ordinarily a primary sore heals in a short time, under a regime of cleanliness and intelligent letting alone, but in cases where septic infections and auto-intoxications from bad dietary practices are pronounced the chancre will show no tendency to heal, but spread and grow more malignant week by week, and in the most severe cases will not heal at all until the system has been brought into a better condition.

The chancre should not be cauterized, nor should any strong ointments be used. The more it is treated this way, the longer it will take to heal. There is one precaution necessary to take in the care of the primary sore, and that is to keep it clean without disturbing it unduly; for bear in mind that we are dealing with a sore that, when not treated right, will cause septic infection. When out of the ordinary, it is made so because of neglect, lack of cleanliness and often very barbarous treatment. Perfect cleanliness from the start will insure a quick and perfect healing.

To remove the secretions, which at times are quite foul and have a characteristic odor, use a little cotton dipped in warm water; or, if an antiseptic is desired, a 1-2000 solution of bichloride may be used. If the parts about the sore are very puffy and tender, they should be bathed two or three times a day in hot water, each bath to last about fifteen minutes.

After the sore is cleansed, it should be dressed so as to cause as little annoyance as possible to the patient while he is working. Each doctor must select the method best suited to the individual

case.   To keep the dressings from adhering, use sterile white vaseline; it is probably as satisfactory as anything.   Powders are
not satisfactory; for when used on large chancres they become
saturated with the exudate and form hard crusts, beneath which
the secretions are held and cause more absorption, and, of course,
more infection.

There are no remedies of greater value in promoting the
healing process than cleanliness without injury to the granulations.
That nature cures has been known for centuries; yet it is not uncommon to hear doctors say:   "I cured an ulcer with this ointment."   Nature does the healing, if she is given the opportunity;
and the less she is interfered with the more quickly she will do the
work.

In treating syphilis, the doctors are too officious.   There is
not much for a doctor to do except to direct the patient.   Teach
him to take care of himself.   This some will not do; for they
fear, if they do not make a great show of doing something, their
patients will feel that they have not earned the fee charged.   The
intelligent class of people will not view things in this light.

The second requisite in treating a neglected or abused primary sore is to give it rest.   On account of the location, this is
often hard to do.   It may be necessary to put the sufferer to bed
for a week or two.   This is better than to have the cure prolonged
for months.

Under the prevailing method of treatment, a patient is not
considered "cured" short of two or three years.   The annoyance,
loss of time and suffering are considerable.   So, if a serious
case has to be put to bed for a week or two, he is not losing
any time; for people who are properly treated and who take good

care of themselves are generally able to do their work at the end of six or eight weeks. Ordinary cases do not have to stay away from their work at all. The rule is that after the first two or three months they can take care of themselves.

The parts can sometimes be given sufficient rest by the use of a T-bandage and the more quiet they are kept, the sooner they heal.

If the primary sore is not maltreated, it will not grow to an enormous size; but sometimes the patient is guilty of wrongdoing and neglect, while at other times the medical treatment is to blame.

The lymphatic glands of the groins sometimes become enormously enlarged (buboes); and especially is this true if what is known as mixed infection has taken place in the primary sore. As has been previously explained, the glands by becoming indurated prevent infection from making rapid progress, and the induration is due to the throwing out of the body's defenses. As soon as the sore is well cleaned and well drained, the tendency for lymphatic enlargement stops and the swelling subsides. When the blood is corrected, the buboes subside. Under proper treatment they soon become so small that they cannot be seen, although they can be felt for a long time.

In a large per cent. of the so-called soft chancre cases treated in the approved fashion, the buboes suppurate, and this is indeed annoying. Cleanliness and good drainage must be had.

Removal of the buboes by the knife is advocated, but it is not satisfactory; for the wound is often reinfected and continues to discharge in spite of the supposed best of care. If the case is properly treated from the start, suppurating buboes need not be feared; in fact, the glands do not enlarge very much. Those people whose intestinal tracts have been foul for years are the ones whose lymphatics swell most.

The average patient dreads the appearance of eruptions on his face most of all. If eliminative treatment is instituted early, the eruptions will not amount to much; if the eruptions are already established, eliminative treatment will soon prevent any further breaking out. When a physician can assure these patients that their hair will not fall out, and that their faces will not show traces of the disease, a great source of worry will be removed. The less one worries, the more quickly will he get well. Some of these people are in a pitiable frame of mind; for they are disgusted with themselves, and they are afraid that they will be disgraced when friends, neighbors and relatives find out their condition. Such a state of mind has to be converted into one of hopefulness and optimism before any great strides in healing can be made.

The eruptions need no special treatment. If they are of the pustular or papulo-pustular variety, they are quite chronic in character and leave colored spots, which fade away in time.

If the patient has a headache—and this is quite common at first—the bowels should be washed out with copious enemas, and no food should be taken till the headache disappears.

The pains in the bones of which so many complain later on are due to malpractice, although malpractice in this case is the approved practice. Medication causes these pains; it also causes other degenerative changes, which the profession groups together under the head of tertiary syphilis.

The popular superstition that this disease is the principal cause of locomotor ataxia is stronger than ever, although it is old and useless enough to be cast aside.

Another superstition which is in daily professional use is that a mild case of syphilis is quite liable to be followed by severe degenerative changes in the various organs of the body, and especially in the spinal cord, where it causes ataxia and the reason given is that these mild cases are not treated long enough. There is absolutely no truth in this statement. The fact of the matter is that the sooner mercurial treatment is given up the better. But if people quit doping and being duped, it means many dollars less in the doctor's pocket; hence the cry for prolonged treatment. The present professional way of conducting syphilitic treatment should be recognized as one of the finest forms of graft known. It is plausible, it is ethical, and it has the approval of nearly all medical men.

Any causes that operate to bring about hardening or degeneration of any part of the body, whether it be a nerve, an artery or the heart wall, may cause locomotor ataxia. There are many fine points in etiology which baffle diagnosticians, but that should not warrant us in declaring that one disease produces another. The fact that the progress of locomotor ataxia can be stayed, and the disease often vastly improved by right living, should prove to an unprejudiced mind that wrong life is at the bottom of this disease, as it is of all others.

With the exception of the primary sore, which should be treated as little as possible, syphilis should not be treated; but the syphilitic should be. Teach him how to live. See to it that he has plenty of fresh air; teach him how to clothe himself, if he does not do it correctly; and by all means teach him how to eat, for here the errors are many and serious.

The average individual has had too much bread, potatoes and meat; he has lived too exclusively on force foods and animal products, and has failed to partake of enough fruits and fresh vegetables. These errors must be corrected. Fresh fruits and vegetables furnish certain salts in which the staple foods are deficient; these salts are necessary for the building of a healthy body. The vegetable and fruit juices act as depurants. The habit of overeating must be conquered.

Constipation must be overcome, if present. If necessary, use an enema every day till the colon is empty. If the constipation is not of long standing, right living will correct it in a very reasonable time.

The use of narcotics and stimulants is both unnecessary and injurious. Tea, coffee, alcoholic drinks and tobacco should not be used. Many will want to quit these habits gradually, but the easiest way to quit is simply to quit. The tapering-off process is accompanied by many disagreeable symptoms, both physical and mental. If tobacco and wrong food habits are stopped at once, in a few days these articles will not be missed much.

A rational treatment, and such I have tried to outline, is indeed very simple; so simple, in fact, that many will think that it cannot be effective in such formidable diseases as syphilis; but the fact is that nature demands no complex treatment. No-where in nature can we find a precedent for the use of compounds of iodin, arsenic and mercury. Nature's order is cleanliness and moderation.

After mercurial treatment many people suffer from symptoms too numerous to mention, varying from skin lesions to deep-seated pains. The orthodox treatment never varies; it is mercurials and iodids. Finally the doctor exhausts all his skill and his patron's patience. What is then to be done? Eureka! Send him to Hot Springs, Arkansas, of course!

Hot Springs is a beautiful little city, taking its name from the numerous springs of hot water that have given the place its reputation. The climate is agreeable and the scenery fine. It is an ideal spot to send people, for they forget their troubles and pay some attention to the beauties of nature. Patients must be—they can't help being favorably impressed—for the place has a great reputation. The government has bathhouses there, and it is the site of a large United States Army and Navy Hospital. This gives the Hot Springs treatment the stamp of official approval.

The baths are supposed to be good for rheumatic and cutaneous disorders. The skin troubles mostly treated are syphilitic lesions. It is the same old treatment, except that here the mercury is given more frequently by inunction than is customary in other places. The only thing new is the change of scene.

A variety of Hot Springs doctors used to have solicitors who went out for some distance to meet the trains, in order to induce the visitors to come to the doctors they represented. Whether this good old custom is yet in vogue the writer does not know. The doctors charge all they think the traffic will bear. Even the most ethical must admit that the members of the medical profession practicing in Hot Springs are thoroughly commercialized.

When a syphilitic goes to see one of these wonderful specialists, whose chief qualifications are that they claim to be specialists, what is known as a course of mercurial treatment, generally by inunction, is prescribed. The number of rubbings to a course, and the number of courses to be gone through, depend upon the prescriber. There are professional rubbers, but those

who cannot afford to pay these men rub each other.   A number
of baths in the spring waters are also prescribed.   The patients
are at liberty to roam about the hills.   One can get very good
accommodations, if he has enough money.   Social features are
a part of the program in the large hotels.   A sort of spirit of
comradery is brought about from the fact that everyone knows
what everyone else has.

The fact is, if it were not for the psychological effects, as
good results could be attained by forgetting business cares, taking
a vacation at home, and using the family bathtub.   This would
have the added advantage of no mercury.   It is all very well for
people of means; but I have met a few who have spent everything
they had for the trip and treatment, after being told by some
doctor that a cure was to be found there.   Of course, they were
disappointed; for in syphilis, as in all other diseases, a cure comes
from within, not from without.   But fakery is part of medical
practice, and will continue to be till the supply of dupes runs out.

What is known as the tertiary stage of syphilis, or the
stage of degeneration, is the result of so-called scientific treatment
and wrong living; for those who are not so treated and live as they
should do not develop into that stage.   Whether these people can
recover or not depends upon the extent to which degenerative
changes have taken place and their willingness to correct their
habits.   It is often possible to stop the progress of the disease
after all cures are supposed to be out of the question.   When degeneration has run into organic change, no regeneration is possible.
But it is safe to say that more can be done for patients by substi-
tuting good habits for their bad ones than by many methods known
as modern medical science.

# INDEX TO GONORRHEA

Page

Abortive treatment . . . . . . . . . . . . . . . . . . . . . . . . . . . . . .13, 57-58
Acidity . . . . . . . . . . . . . . . . . . . . . . . . . . . . . . . . . . . . . . . .18-20
Adepts in vice . . . . . . . . . . . . . . . . . . . . . . . . . . . . . . . . . . . . 62
Alkalinity . . . . . . . . . . . . . . . . . . . . . . . . . . . . . . . . . . . . . . . . 18

Bath for orchitis . . . . . . . . . . . . . . . . . . . . . . . . . . . . . . . . . . . 44
Bending of penis . . . . . . . . . . . . . . . . . . . . . . . . . . . . . . . . . . . 65
Bladder, inflammation of . . . . . . . . . . . . . . . . . . . . . . . . . . .34, 41
    Irrigation . . . . . . . . . . . . . . . . . . . . . . . . . . . . . . . . . . . . . . 41
    Use only warm distilled water . . . .  –  . . . . . . . . . . . . . . . . . 42
    When to irrigate . . . . . . . . . . . . . . . . . . . . . . . . . . . . . . . . . 41
Bubo . . . . . . . . . . . . . . . . . . . . . . . . . . . . . . . . . . . . . . . . . . . 51
    Causes of . . . . . . . . . . . . . . . . . . . . . . . . . . . . . . . . . . . . . . 51
    Treatment of . . . . . . . . . . . . . . . . . . . . . . . . . . . . . . . . . .51-52

Catheter, when to use . . . . . . . . . . . . . . . . . . . . . . . . . . . . . . . 40
Cause and effect . . . . . . . . . . . . . . . . . . . . . . . . . . . . . . . . . . . 8
Character of disease . . . . . . . . . . . . . . . . . . . . . . . . . . . . . . . . 29
Characteristic diseases . . . . . . . . . . . . . . . . . . . . . . . . . . . . . . 29
Charges . . . . . . . . . . . . . . . . . . . . . . . . . . . . . . . . . . . . . . . . . 16
Chordee . . . . . . . . . . . . . . . . . . . . . . . . . . . . . . . . . . . . . . . . . 65
Circumcision . . . . . . . . . . . . . . . . . . . . . . . . . . . . . . . . . . . . . . 6
Cleanliness . . . . . . . . . . . . . . . . . . . . . . . . . . . . . . . . . . . . . . . 37
Clothes, their influence . . . . . . . . . . . . . . . . . . . . . . . . . . . . . . 7
Complications, cause of . . . . . . . . . . . . . . . . . . . . . . . . . . . . . . 38
Control the patient . . . . . . . . . . . . . . . . . . . . . . . . . . . . . . .16-17
Critics do not know . . . . . . . . . . . . . . . . . . . . . . . . . . . . . . . . 10
Cures, the three-day . . . . . . . . . . . . . . . . . . . . . . . . . . . . . . . . 11
Curse of civilization . . . . . . . . . . . . . . . . . . . . . . . . . . . . . . . . 8
Customary dressings . . . . . . . . . . . . . . . . . . . . . . . . . . . . . . . . 37

Decomposition . . . . . . . . . . . . . . . . . . . . . . . . . . . . . . . . . . . . 33
Diet . . . . . . . . . . . . . . . . . . . . . . . . . . . . . . . . . . . . . . . . .33, 37
Discharge, when it is great . . . . . . . . . . . . . . . . . . . . . . . . . . . . 36
Diseases, special types of . . . . . . . . . . . . . . . . . . . . . . . . . . . . 24
    Prolonging . . . . . . . . . . . . . . . . . . . . . . . . . . . . . . . . . . . . . 35
Dormant, germs lie . . . . . . . . . . . . . . . . . . . . . . . . . . . . . . . . . 61
Drainage of wounds . . . . . . . . . . . . . . . . . . . . . . . . . . . . . .24, 38
    Free . . . . . . . . . . . . . . . . . . . . . . . . . . . . . . . . . . . . . . . . . 37
    Imperfect . . . . . . . . . . . . . . . . . . . . . . . . . . . . . . . . . . . . . . 26

|  | Page |
|---|---|
| Dressing for gonorrhea | 36-37 |
| Dressings, obstructive | 37-39 |
| Drinks to be avoided | 14 |
| Drugless treatment | 10 |
| Drugs mask symptoms | 10 |
| Epididymitis | 43 |
| Treatment of | 43 |
| Erysipelas | 21 |
| Excitement, sexual | 55-56 |
| Fasting, importance of | 33, 54, 59 |
| Fees by the month | 16 |
| In advance | 16 |
| Fluids of the body | 20 |
| Food, amount of | 14, 37 |
| Influence of | 60 |
| Kind of | 14 |
| Foreskin, swelling of | 33 |
| Germs, their habitat | 23 |
| Glands, influence of mercury on | 19 |
| Gleet | 53 |
| Quick cure of | 54 |
| Gonorrhea, abortive treatment of | 13 |
| Badly managed | 12 |
| Chronic | 53 |
| Dressing for | 35 |
| Gentle treatment of | 13, 35 |
| In women | 63 |
| Marriage in | 56 |
| Recurrence of | 55 |
| Reinfection in | 56 |
| Specific treatment of | 35 |
| Treatment of | 35 |
| Greeks | 6 |
| Hunter, John | 7 |
| Hygienic treatment | 14 |
| Immunity | 64 |
| Infection, contact | 32, 64 |
| Danger of | 62 |
| Modes of | 32 |
| No immunity from | 64 |

Infection—Continued                                                    Page
    Of prostates .................. .......................... 40
    Unity of .................. .. ......... ...... ......... 18
Inflammation.................................... ........ 24
    Endings of ............................................ 25
    Simple and specific.................... ... .........24, 30
Interchangeableness of infection.................. .    ...    ... 22

Jews........................................................ 6

Keyes, Dr. E. L.................... ... .. .. ........11-15
King David .......................................  . ...... 5

Latent symptoms ........................................ 28
Lymphatic glands ...................................... 20
    Inflammation of .......................................... 51

Masturbation..................................... ...... 45
Meat................................................... 40
Meatus plugging up.................................. ... 39
Mercury, influence of.................................. 19
Mind must be free from sex thoughts............................ 15
    Its influence ............................................ 89
Mucous membrane. in inflammation................. 24
    Granular thickening of ..... .. ............................ 48

Obstructive dressings...... ............ ...............37-39
Olive-tipped sound ...................................46-66
Orchitis................................. .. .........34-43
    Suppuration in .......................................... 44
    Treatment of .............................. .. .... 44
Overeating, its influence.................. ..  .   ...... 59

Pasteur............................................ ...... 9
Patients must be controlled...................................... 16
Pay in advance............................................. 16
Pent-up discharge ...................................... 26
Peril of venereal diseases.................................... 31
Physicians, ignorant or dishonest................... ......... 11
    Seldom infected .......................................... 58
Pleasure to treat venereal diseases............................. 17
Prevention of disease.... ...................................... 6
    By primitive habits................................ . ........ 7
Preventive treatment ...................................57-58
Prostate gland .......................................34-40
Prostatitis........................................... ...... 40

|                                                          | Page   |
|----------------------------------------------------------|--------|
| Reaction of body fluids                                  | 18     |
| Recurrence, causes of                                    | 55     |
| Relationship of specific diseases                        | 25     |
| Resistance, great in a few                               | 59     |
| Rest, need of                                            | 24     |
| Rhus. tox.                                               | 21     |
| Scientific Congress                                      | 9      |
| Self-limitation of gonorrhea                             | 61     |
| Sepsis, virulent                                         | 26     |
| Septic absorption                                        | 27     |
| Sexual excitement                                        | 55-56  |
| Skin disease                                             | 28     |
| Smoking, sepsis                                          | 23     |
| Soldiers and venereal disease                            | 7      |
| Sound, olive-tipped                                      | 46     |
| Rubbing with                                             | 47     |
| Specific infection is septic                             | 30     |
| Spirocheta pallida                                       | 8      |
| Sterility                                                | 43     |
| Stricture                                                | 45     |
| How to treat                                             | 46     |
| How to use the sound                                     | 46-47  |
| Location of                                              | 46     |
| Organic                                                  | 48     |
| Treatment of                                             | 49     |
| Swelling of foreskin                                     | 33     |
| Of mucous membrane                                       | 24     |
| Towel, advantage of wearing                              | 36     |
| How to wear                                              | 36     |
| Treatment, of chordee                                    | 65-66  |
| Of gonorrhea in men                                      | 35     |
| Of gonorrhea in women                                    | 63     |
| Present plan of                                          | 37     |
| Types of contagious diseases, the worst                  | 8      |
| Urethritis, simple                                       | 23     |
| Specific                                                 | 23     |
| Venereal diseases are skin diseases                      | 28     |
| Virulent sepsis                                          | 26     |
| Wasserman test                                           | 39     |
| Women of easy virtue                                     | 62     |
| Treatment of gonorrhea in                                | 63     |
| Wounds and venereal treatment                            | 8      |

# INDEX TO SYPHILIS

|  | Page |
|---|---|
| A case | 125 |
| Acid secretions | 135 |
| After infection | 133 |
| Aristocratic maladies | 118 |
| Arsenic | 114, 157 |
| Auto-infection, treatment of | 98 |
| Autotoxemia | 129 |
|   Cause of all diseases | 72 |
|   Causes of | 73 |
|   Cure of | 73 |
| Bathing, directions for | 103 |
| Beliefs, appropriated without credit | 127 |
|   Malicious | 128 |
|   Numbers make respectable | 127 |
| Bone lesions | 136 |
| Bread, Tilden toast | 104 |
| Building the disease | 138 |
| Cause, if not understood | 128 |
|   Must be known | 128 |
| Chancroid | 79, 90, 100 |
|   Treatment of | 101 |
| Chaotic reasoning | 113 |
| Chronic syphilis | 116 |
| Cleanliness | 74 |
| Compensation | 138 |
| Consolation | 128 |
| Constipation | 106 |
|   Foods that produce | 106 |
|   Its influence | 123, 134 |
| Cures, a delusion | 113 |
|   Apparent | 122 |
|   Die hard | 123 |
|   Nature's | 111 |
|   On the spot | 113 |
|   Require time | 111 |
|   Snapshot | 111 |
|   "606" | 113 |

|  | Page |
|---|---|
| Development, complex | 117 |
| Diagnosis by exclusion | 145 |
| Diarrhea | 76 |
| Discoveries, profession frenzied by | 115 |
|   Widely heralded | 122 |
| Disease, blood | 112 |
|   Disreputable | 118 |
|   Individuality of | 112 |
|   Is caused by | 111 |
| Diseases are mistaken | 118 |
| Doctors give no information | 119 |
| Drugs cause skin trouble | 155 |
|   Do not cure | 162 |
|   Mask symptoms | 86 |
| Eating, rules for | 105 |
| Ehrlich, Dr. Paul | 112 |
| Elixir of life | 115 |
|   Believed in by the profession | 115 |
| Eminent specialists | 138 |
| Eruptions | 83 |
|   Should be classified | 156 |
| Etiology or cause, not advanced | 128 |
| Fear | 89, 92, 135, 165 |
| Fever | 77, 140 |
| Find what you look for | 147 |
| Foods, combinations of | 107 |
|   Constipating | 106 |
|   Decidedly starchy | 105 |
|   Mastication of | 106 |
|   Non-starchy | 104 |
| Formulary | 103-109 |
| Genitals, care of | 101 |
| Germ theory a mind-saver | 129 |
| Germs | 129 |
|   A necessity | 130 |
|   Killed in the blood | 113 |
| Glands, lymphatic | 124 |
| Glandular involvement | 83 |
| Gumma | 143 |

Page

Hair, loss of............................................34, 142
Hard chancre .................................................  80
  Its cause ...............................................80, 81
Headaches.................................................... 140
Herxheimer test .............................................. 166

If what we believe isn't true.................................. 128
Impotency....................................................  92
Infant mortality ............................................. 167
Infection, deep...........................................32, 75
  Superficial..............................................  75
Information, doctors give none............................... 119
  Magazines give ......................................... 119
  Newspapers give......................................... 119
  Public gets ............................................ 119
Initial abrasion ............................................ 125
Introduction................................................  71
Iodine salts ................................................ 121
Iritis.......................................................  84

Jaw-bones destroyed by mercury............................... 151
Jew, why he suffers less..................................... 132

Law of compensation.......................................... 138
Life, beautiful ............................................. 117
  Is it vulgar or obscene?................................ 117
Locomotor ataxia .........................................85, 144
Logic of medicine............................................ 121
Lymphatic glands ............................................ 124

Malicious beliefs ........................................... 128
  Influence............................................... 128
Malpractice.................................................. 151
Masticating food ............................................ 106
Meats, classes of............................................ 107
Mercury and blood-letting. .................................. 151
  And starch poison....................................... 116
  Causes loss of teeth.................................... 120
  Causes necrosis ........................................ 121
  Destroys jaw-bone ...................................... 151
  Diseases produced by.................................... 124
  Dr. King's explanation.................................. 152
  In syphilis ............................................  96
  Its administration ..................................... 154

(185)

| | Page |
|---|---|
| Mercury—Continued | |
| Its sheet-anchor | 113 |
| Jaw-bones destroyed | 151 |
| Kills the germ | 121 |
| Mouth and throat, effects of | 151 |
| Salivation | 118, 120 |
| Specific | 121 |
| Used 400 years ago | 120 |
| Why it salivates | 136 |
| Mixed infection | 79 |
| Mucous patches | 84 |
| | |
| Nerve degeneration | 91 |
| New discoveries | 115 |
| Non-starchy vegetables | 104 |
| | |
| Pathology | 136 |
| Peasant girl's case | 164 |
| People, two classes of | 131 |
| Peril, the venereal | 31 |
| Poisoning, septic | 76, 77, 112 |
| Popular side | 127 |
| Prevention | 123 |
| Primary sore | 132 |
| Profession should feel proud | 144 |
| Public will outgrow the present belief | 118 |
| Puzzle, syphilis a | 119 |
| | |
| Question of several hundred years ago | 137 |
| Questioner silenced | 137 |
| | |
| Remedies, two roads to their discovery | 111 |
| Remove all causes | 77 |
| Rest a remedy | 138 |
| Rules, the four | 105-106 |
| | |
| Salad, the Tilden | 107 |
| Salivation | 97 |
| Salvarsan in syphilis (see Six-hundred-and-six) | 157 |
| One dose of | 167 |
| Scrofula | 112 |
| Septic inflammation | 30 |
| Septic poisoning | 76, 77, 112 |
| Serums | 129 |
| Simple and septic inflammation | 30 |
| "Six-hundred-and-six" | 112, 114-116, 119, 121, 124, 147, 156-157 |

|  |  | Page |
|---|---|---|
| Skin, an index | | 142 |
| Diseases, the four varieties | | 141 |
| Cause of | | 73 |
| Cure of | | 74 |
| Eruptions | | 141 |
| Mucous and bone lesion in | | 136 |
| Soft chancre | | 100 |
| Treatment of | | 101 |
| Soup, vegetable | | 164 |
| Specifics | | 111-116, 121 |
| The three | | 120 |
| Starchy foods | | 105 |
| Susceptibility of a few | | 134 |
| Symptomatology | | 136 |
| Syphilis, a filth disease primarily | | 123 |
| A lie | | 72 |
| A modern disease | | 119 |
| A puzzle | | 119 |
| A severe course | | 133 |
| A skin disease | | 72 |
| A typhoid case | | 120 |
| As I have found it | | 88 |
| Causation | | 127 |
| Caused by a germ | | 120 |
| Chronic | | 116 |
| Contagiousness of | | 71 |
| Curability of | | 116 |
| Definition of | | 75 |
| Doctors build | | 138 |
| Hard to diagnose | | 144 |
| How infection takes place | | 123 |
| Ignorance of | | 117 |
| In the Middle Ages | | 120 |
| Initial lesion in | | 125 |
| Laymen ignorant of | | 118 |
| No prehistoric signs of | | 137 |
| Not specific | | 82 |
| Of the nervous system | | 90 |
| Origin of | | 71 |
| Reasons for variation of | | 136 |
| Should be discussed | | 118 |
| Society honeycombed with | | 114 |
| Symptoms | | 124 |
| A protest | | 138 |

Syphilis—Continued                                              Page
   Tertiary.............................................................. 143
   The nemesis ........................................................ 114
   Theory wrong ...................................................... 79
   Three stages in.................................................... 139
   Versatility of ...................................................... 136
   Young men and young women should know..................... 117

Teakettle tea ........................................................... 107
Teeth fall out.......................................................... 149
Tertiary symptoms .................................................... 143
Tilden salad............................................................ 107
Tilden toast bread, how to make................................... 104
Treatment...................................................94, 124, 148, 169
   Of a cure........................................................... 125
   Of auto-infection ................................................. 98
   Of locomotor ataxia.............................................. 91
Tubercular bacillus ................................................... 130
Typhoid fever ......................................................... 76

Unborn generations ................................................... 126
Uncleanliness.......................................................... 133

Vampire................................................................. 119
Vegetable soup ........................................................ 104
Vegetables, laxative .................................................. 106
   Non-starchy........................................................ 104
Vulgar or obscene..................................................... 117

Wassermann's test ...............................................145, 162
   Proves nothing ................................................... 146
Water, when to drink................................................ 106
"Whited sepulchers" .................................................. 123
Why "606" gives more satisfaction................................. 122
Worry.................................................................. 142

CPSIA information can be obtained
at www.ICGtesting.com
Printed in the USA
BVOW04s0236101117
499866BV00052BA/784/P